# "I'll Get You!"

Drugs, Lies, and the Terrorizing of a PTA Mom

## Riley J. Ford & Kelli Peters

Copyright © 2016 Riley J. Ford & Kelli Peters
Print Edition

All rights reserved. No part of this book may be reproduced in any form or by electronic or mechanical means, including information storage and retrieval systems—except in the case of brief quotations embodied in critical articles or reviews—without permission in writing from the author.

This book is dedicated to my superhuman family. If you were in any way involved in helping us stand up to the Easter Monster, or just helping us stand up, then you are my family. Bill: Thank you, sweetheart, for your love and gentleness. Sydnie: Thank you, my love, for your humor and spunk. Because of you, I survived. ~Peace, Kelli

This book is dedicated to Dina and JD. You know why. ~Riley

Special thanks to our beta readers: Ana, Cassie, Chris, Christy, Janette, Josh, Kathie, Mannie, Miki, Perry, and Tina. This book is better because of you. A special shout-out to Chris from RCS for letting us work by the pool. ~R & K

# foreword

On February 17, 2010, an Orange County mother and attorney named Jill Easter accused a longtime PTA volunteer, Kelli Peters, of deliberately locking her son out of an afterschool program. This was not true. Nevertheless, the misunderstanding began five years of what Kelli Peters describes as "a campaign of torture" against her that involved gossip, lies, threats, lawsuits, and the planting of drugs on an innocent person. It ended with a conviction against Jill Easter and her attorney husband, Kent, for their crimes against PTA mom Kelli Peters. Jill Easter took a plea deal and spent four months in prison. Kent Easter was convicted of a felony and spent six months in jail. After the felony conviction against the Easters, Kelli Peter won a civil lawsuit for emotional damages that resulted in a judgment of $5.7 million against the Easters.

How and why did all of this begin?

When I first heard about this case, before I knew the players involved and the details of the story, I thought it was a sensational tabloid story about two women caught up in a catfight that escalated out of control. It conjured up images of the Real Housewives and all of their drama and wineglass throwing. I thought, as many people think when they first hear about this story, that the victim in this case, Kelli Peters, must have done *something* to Jill Easter to set her off and cause her such visceral rage. After all, the adage "there are two sides to every story" exists for a reason. Indeed, there is also Jill's story in this case. I'm sure she has her own perspective on what happened that caused her to make the choices she made, no matter how deluded some may think it is.

But this book is not about Jill Easter. Nor is it about Kent Easter, Jill's husband, the man who went along with her plan to "get" Kelli Peters, even though he'd never once met the PTA volunteer in his life.

This book is about Kelli, the woman I came to know as I wrote her story: an ordinary woman with a kind heart; a woman who, up until this point, had lived a peaceful life. She always chose to see the positive in every situation. She gave fully of herself to her family, friends, and community. She rescued animals and volunteered with children. She was happy…until one day she inexplicably found herself in the crosshairs of someone she'd never met before, a woman hellbent on destruction and, in Kelli's words, "mentally unstable and evil."

The first thing people always asked me when they found out I was writing this book was: "What was the motive?" Indeed, I searched long and hard for the true motives behind Jill and Kent Easter's crimes. I interviewed the criminal prosecutor, the civil prosecutor, Kelli's co-volunteers and friends, people at the school who were there that day, and Kelli herself. I read court transcripts and asked questions and delved into the issue. No one could come up with a solid, concrete motive for why Jill Easter decided to go after Kelli Peters.

There were plenty of theories, yes, some of which will be explored in this book. But what it really comes down to is this: sometimes bad things happen to good people without explanation. Inexplicable events can unfold in our lives with no rhyme or reason. Sometimes people are targeted by others without cause. We can incur tragedy or hardship or trauma in our lives through no fault of our own. Good, innocent people die in car accidents at the hands of negligent people.

Decent, law-abiding people are cheated on, lied to, swindled, and harmed. It happens every day. As human beings, we always seek to find out the "why" for an unthinkable occurrence in the lives of others in the hopes we can avoid the harm ourselves.

But sometimes, no matter how carefully or honorably we live our lives, there is no avoiding the lightning bolt out of the sky. There is no predicting the unpredictable, especially when it comes to random criminal behavior or the actions of other people who may wish us harm.

Oftentimes, we never see it coming.

We are blindsided, our lives forever changed due to a chance meeting of fate.

That is what happened to Kelli Peters.

This is her story.

—Riley J. Ford

*Statement from Dr. Nina Rodd, Ph.D., who treated Kelli Peters throughout her ordeal with the Easters:*

I saw my role as the provider of healing for the deep fear and traumatic wounds that Kelli and her family had sustained. This meant that I was an instrument of help. I had to evaluate the needs of my patient and determine how I could provide her with either the therapeutic techniques or guide her to get the necessary help from other sources.

My role was to empower a woman who felt helpless, hopeless, fearful for her own life and her family's life, and who was totally devastated. My patient not only trusted me and accepted help, she also was appreciative of the assistance I was providing to her and her family.

Kelli saw her life, her safety, her reputation, and her daughter's life being threatened and destroyed in just one day, maybe in a few hours, or only in a few minutes. She saw her life and her family's life ruined. After that infamous day she still didn't know: If she was going to jail? Would police find her innocent or not? What else this woman and her husband are capable of doing. How far would they go with their violent behavior? It wasn't only the posttraumatic stress disorder and its devastating symptoms that she was suffering from. She was realistically living on an hourly basis, a nightmare of what else was going to happen to her, her daughter or her husband. Sleepless nights, nightmares every time she fell asleep, hypervigilance, being startled at any little noise or event, anxiety, thought rumination, and withdrawing from her world and her friends are just some of the things she was suffering on a daily basis.

I am a clinical and forensic psychologist. I have evaluated hundreds of trauma cases and have provided psychological treatment to many of them on their way to healing. My main observation in all of those trauma cases has been that the deep wounds of PTSD don't go away. With treatment and passage of time, the symptoms get dimmed, but they are waiting in the shadows until another trauma or stressful event occurs and ignites them again. It has been meaningful for me to testify to the lifelong effects of PTSD in patients that I have evaluated and treated, and to make it known that the nightmare leaves its footprint in the soul of the patient.

I diagnosed the family with the following:

Kelli: Posttraumatic stress disorder and generalized anxiety disorder.

Sydnie: Posttraumatic stress disorder.

Bill: Initially an acute trauma disorder, generalized anxiety disorder, and followed with major depressive disorder.

I have not personally evaluated Jill Easter, so I don't have any opinion about her diagnosis. Since there has been mention of the psychopathic personality in regard to this case, I listed some of the criteria for antisocial personality disorder as they appear in *Diagnostic and Statistical Manual of Mental Disorders-V* as follows:

- Failure to conform to social norms with respect to lawful behaviors.
- Deceitfulness, as indicated by repeated lying, use of aliases, or conning others for personal profit or pleasure.
- Reckless disregard for safety of self or others.
- Lack of remorse, as indicated by being indifferent to or rationalizing having hurt, mistreated, or stolen from others.

We are all exposed to the reckless behavior of those who may be psychopaths. They are out there in our everyday life. They cover it over and come in different colors, shapes, genders, professions, and levels of education. Kelli was trusting, loving, positive, and she disbelieved in the level of evilness of someone who came to interact with her just for a few minutes, whose evil behavior changed Kelli's life forever. Kelli took charge of her life and tried to heal herself and eventually even empowered herself.

In this book she is now sharing her healing and empowerment with all of those who may have befallen victims to such an individual's threats and actions in similar situations.

—Dr. Nina Rodd, Ph.D.

# one

On the afternoon of February 17, 2011, a vanilla PT Cruiser pulled into the parking lot of Plaza Vista Elementary School in Irvine, California. Just beyond the school, large jacaranda trees swayed lightly in the breeze, soon to drop delicate purple flowers on the suburban streets and turn the sidewalks into a dusty purple carpet. This was Irvine, a place as idyllic as they come. This was a town where crime was nearly nonexistent. In fact, in 2015, Irvine was voted the safest large city in the U.S. by the FBI—for the eleventh consecutive year in a row.

Southern California is a place of many identities. There is the bustling area of Hollywood where movie deals are made over five-hundred-dollar lunches. There is Manhattan Beach, where college students both live and commute to nearby colleges or downtown. There are the inner cities where residents live behind barred windows, fighting to survive amidst flying bullets and circling helicopters. California is the land of the haves and have-nots, and this is seen most starkly in the upper middle-class enclave of Irvine, forty-five miles south of Los Angeles.

When describing Orange County, people often say that those who live there exist "behind the Orange curtain." This describes the sense that one is leaving the frenetic pace of Los Angeles and entering the

Land of Oz. Irvine is a city known for its seeming perfection, with its pristine, clean streets and manicured lawns. As a master-planned community, everything caters to those who wish to bring their children up in a safe, tranquil place. There are green belts, community pools, brand-new shopping centers, and well-maintained gas stations on accessible corners. The community is known for its excellent schools. For example, University High in Irvine, a gold medal school, was recently voted one of the best high schools in the country by U.S. News. The average home price in Irvine is $780,000, according to Zillow in June of 2016. Even townhomes look like resorts, with beautiful pools, landscaped gardens, and workout rooms.

The blonde woman who exited the PT Cruiser, Kelli Peters, was thankful to be able to live and raise her daughter in a place like Irvine. Sometimes she couldn't believe her good fortune to be able to provide a desirable suburban life for her daughter, despite not being a person of wealth. She and her husband lived in a modest apartment and watched every penny so she could stay home with Sydnie. As a parent volunteer, Kelli got to spend her afternoons at the school with her daughter and the other sweet children who attended Plaza Vista Elementary School. For a mom who loved kids, what could be better than that?

Kelli headed through the parking lot toward the school. She was looking forward to her afternoon, as she always did when she arrived at Plaza Vista, her second home. As coordinator for the afterschool classroom enrichment program, or ACE, she had a lot to do. She looked after a multitude of kids, all enrolled in a variety of programs, from cooking to tennis. She was responsible for making sure everything ran well and that the children were happy and cared for. She also helped the teachers in whatever capacity they needed her.

Kelli's favorite program was the one she oversaw directly, the art program that was funded by the PTA. She was partial to this program because her daughter loved art and had been immersed in it since she was a young child. Kelli loved getting the art supplies ready every day for the students, setting up the classroom, and seeing the eager faces of the children as they entered through the doors. She never tired of greeting them or giving them hugs. She never tired of helping them learn about art. Most of all, Kelli loved being able to spend time with her ten-year-old daughter, Sydnie. She adored all of the kids in the program, but getting to hang out with her little girl was the highlight of her day. She'd begun volunteering when Syd was in kindergarten, and now here it was, five years later. She knew just about everyone: kids, parents, and administrators alike. There was a reason Plaza Vista Elementary School had become like a family to Kelli and her daughter.

As Kelli headed into the building, her heart ballooned with joy. Life seemed perfect at that moment. Sure, she had problems like everyone else, but nothing she couldn't manage. She was happily married, had a close relationship with her parents, enjoyed the company of many good friends, worked in a fulfilling volunteer position where she felt valued and needed, and got to spend time with her beautiful little girl every day. She had everything she needed.

Little did Kelli know that in a few short moments, her life was about to change forever.

An hour later, she was called out of the afterschool program and told by an administrator that there were police there to see her.

When Kelli arrived at the administrator's office, an Irvine police officer approached her and said that someone had reported her for erratic driving and drug possession.

The officer marched her to her PT Cruiser, which was blocked by a police car. A helicopter swirled overhead.

Kelli gasped to see a large bag of marijuana in plain sight on the back seat of her car behind the driver's seat. There were also baggies of pills, along with a crack pipe.

The officers pulled the drugs and paraphernalia out of Kelli's vehicle and placed them on top of their police car in plain view of parents, administrators, and children.

"Those drugs aren't mine!" Kelli protested. She began to sob. "Please take them off the car. The kids can't see them. My daughter can't see them!"

"If the drugs aren't yours," one of the officers said, "then how did they get there?"

"Someone must've planted them!"

"Who could have done that? Do you have any enemies?"

Kelli paused as a realization began to dawn on her.

"Yes, actually, I do have an enemy."

"What is this person's name?"

"Jill Easter."

The officers wrote down the name.

Kelli began to tremble all over. Yes, it made sense.

*Jill Easter.*

Jill had to have had a hand in this. Who else would do something so vicious, so evil?

Of course.

No one else but Jill Easter.

A year earlier to the day, she'd met Jill for the first and only time. There was a misunderstanding between the two women that ended with Jill screaming at the top of her lungs, "I'll get you!" at Kelli's retreating back.

Kelli's throat clenched at the memory of those words. Jill had shouted that phrase in such a chilling tone that shivers had gone down her spine, and she'd had nightmares about it ever since.

It seemed Jill Easter was now making good on her threat.

*I'll get you!*

Today was February 17…a year to the day since her original confrontation with Jill. There were now drugs mysteriously planted in Kelli's car. That date couldn't be a coincidence.

# two

Suburban moms are not immune to being in the news. Consider the cases of Pamela Smart, the teacher who coerced a student into murdering her husband. Or Wanda Holloway, the Texas mother who hired a hitman to take out a rival cheerleader mom in the hopes of securing a spot for her daughter on the cheerleading team.

Being a homemaker who carpools and bakes cookies doesn't guarantee a peaceful existence. Nor does it assure normalcy. In fact, in some cases, the identity of mother and homemaker is a façade that an ambitious woman might hide behind. The children may be used as pawns to further the agenda of a woman who might have previously used her skills to succeed in the workplace. Raw ambition doesn't relegate itself to the boardrooms of the world. As any mother will attest, sometimes the most blatantly ambitious people can be found in the schools and suburban neighborhoods of America.

It may be a small percentage of women who operate in this way, but they are easily recognizable in cities all over the nation. She's the mother who shows up at the school dressed to the nines with her hair blow-dried to perfection and a full face of makeup. She might be the kind of woman who has two nannies so she can run her errands of Botox, mani-pedis, and lunchtime massages instead of grocery shopping or picking her kids up on time from school. She might be the type who will gossip about other women she finds a threat, spreading rumors and lies if she has to. She's a master at psychological warfare to bring down any woman who she views as competition. She will brag about her children being the best, and God help them if they are not. She is often called a "helicopter mom" behind her back by the teachers exasperated with her high-maintenance stance and overbearing attitude. She will do anything to make sure that her children get ahead and reflect well on her, because it really isn't about the children at all.

It's about competition. It's about winning.

At Plaza Vista Elementary School, as in any school, these kinds of women exist.

Kelli Peters, as described by the people who knew her, was not one of these women.

In fact, she was the opposite of high maintenance and demanding.

"She's more like an earth-mother-hippie-beach girl," her friend Monique says. "She's very real and hardworking. She always goes with the flow. She has a peace sign on her car for a reason."

Kelli would more likely be seen running around wearing John Lennon sunglasses and gauzy baby-doll dresses than sporting five-hundred-dollar jeans and designer shoes.

As the daughter of a waitress/horse trainer and an insurance salesman/drummer, Kelli valued hard work and living modestly. She'd worked all her life starting at a young age, along with caring for her three younger brothers while her parents worked night shifts.

Kelli never complained, though. In fact, she enjoyed hard work. "I've always loved staying busy," she says. "It's where I find much of my happiness. I like feeling productive."

Of course, Kelli had her faults, like anyone. She was too trusting, to the point that she was often caught off guard by overbearing people. She didn't know how to play "the game" with those certain women who sometimes had an agenda hidden behind their cheery smiles. Kelli's mother would say, "You're too nice. One day it's going to bite you in the butt."

Jill Easter was a law school graduate and former attorney. Her parents lived in one of the wealthiest neighborhoods in Newport Beach. Jill herself lived in a million-dollar home in Irvine.

Outside observers described her as an ice queen: stoic, standoffish, and inaccessible. Although some people thought she was self-righteous and smug, she could be socially friendly under the right circumstances.

But, as one Plaza Vista mom noted, "She always seemed to be sizing everyone up."

Jill took her appearance seriously. She wore the current trends, but they were slightly oversized, as if she were hiding something. She was tall and attractive in the typical well-groomed Orange County way. She had large white teeth, full lips (some said enhanced), smooth skin, and long blonde hair that rarely showed dark roots. She had deep dimples when she smiled, which was rare. Later, her look would change, become more plastic and enhanced, but in 2010, she was what people would consider an attractive woman.

"I thought she was very pretty," Kelli says. "She was confident and well dressed. She seemed to have it all."

One got the sense that Jill Easter knew she was attractive and used it to her advantage. She also had a law degree, something she let people know immediately upon meeting them.

"She seemed like a woman who was used to getting her way," Kelli's friend Monique says. "I thought she was a bit of a spoiled brat. I doubt she was told no very often."

There was no denying that Jill Easter had a certain strange allure. Some might call it charisma; others might describe it as a dark intensity. Still others might say it was the way she carried herself, as if she were a queen playing to the public. Whatever it was, it both drew people to Jill and repelled them.

"I think it was the look in her icy blue eyes," Kelli says. "Some people might have found them intriguing, but I thought they were scary."

In any case, there was no denying that most people knew who Jill Easter was wherever she went. She made an impression, whether good or bad, and people never forgot her.

Despite their differences in how they related to people, Kelli and Jill did have some commonalities. They were both blonde and attractive. They'd both grown up in the same area. They both had children at Plaza Vista Elementary School. They were both married suburban housewives. And they were both, by all accounts and purposes, devoted to their children.

That devotion expressed itself in different ways, as it always does with parents. There are as many parenting styles among people as there are grains of sand along the Newport Beach boardwalk. Volunteering in the classroom, carpooling, making wholesome lunches, and shuttling their kids to afterschool activities are all in a typical day's work for many suburban parents. Some moms are known for micromanaging their children's lives down to the detail, ensuring they have the best of everything no matter what it takes. "Tiger mom," "mama bear," or "helicopter mom" are descriptions of these kinds of women for a reason.

*"Don't get in the way of Ms. Helicopter Parent! That overprotective mama bear will raise hell if little Johnny snowflake doesn't get an A in basket weaving."*

By all accounts, Kelli Peters and Jill Easter were two very different examples of a typical Orange County mother.

And on a fateful day in 2010, one year before the drugs were planted in Kelli Peters' car, their paths crossed.

Their lives, and those of their children and families, would be changed forever. Loss, loss, and more loss would follow.

There would be no winners.

# three

**Kelli** remembers her childhood as idyllic. "It was such a happy time," she recalls. "We were a very close-knit family."

Her mother Kathy was a blackjack dealer at Harrah's Casino when she met Bob Storms, who was a drummer in a rock and roll band called The Band. After dating for a few years, they decided to marry.

Kelli Storms was born on September 14, 1961 in Reno, Nevada.

Kelli's younger brother, Bill, was born a year later.

When Kelli was three, her family moved from Reno to the San Gabriel Valley in California, where her mother began working as a "pony girl" caring for horses at the local racetrack. She later worked as a cocktail waitress. Mr. Storms was an insurance agent by day to support his family and played in his band on the weekends. For the first seven years of Kelli's life, Bob Storms would go on tour. Kelli, her mom, and Bill would often go with him. They would pack up and drive to Seattle, Las Vegas, and other places on the West Coast. During that time, The Band played quite a few gigs and even cut some albums.

"It was such a fun adventure," Kelli remembers. "I always loved traveling with my parents. It was exciting. My dad loves to tell a story about whenever we would go to Seattle, my brother Bill and I thought we were going to see a guy named Addle. We would get very excited about going to see Addle, jumping up and down and screaming with joy. My dad didn't have the heart to tell us there was no such person as Addle, so everyone just kind of played along for years."

Kelli was the only girl and the oldest child of three brothers: Bill, Bobby, and Kevin.

"Growing up in a houseful of boys was interesting," she says. "There were always antics going on."

They were an active family. Mr. Storms loved sports and had played college baseball, so he loved coaching his sons' baseball and football teams. He coached Kelli's softball team as well. Kelli was also a cheerleader for Little League and football, and would cheer for her brother Bill's team. She also took a dance class once a week: jazz, ballet, and tap. Kelli took that class from the time she was six years old until in high school.

"I can't dance to save my life," she says, laughing. "My family likes to joke that I took all those years of ballet and still don't have an ounce of rhythm. My dance team would get asked to dance at the fair every year. My dad took many videos of me dancing on stage and literally going the wrong direction or tripping in front of everyone."

"All those years of ballet…!" Mr. and Mrs. Storms would say, exchanging rueful glances and shaking their heads in exasperation.

"I was a huge tomboy," Kelli says, "so I think my mom was hoping to instill some sort of poise and grace in me… I'd like to think she succeeded, but I still can't dance to save my life."

Although dance was enjoyable, Kelli's favorite activity was going to visit her boarded horse with her mother. Her mom had ridden horses since she was a child, and had a deep affinity for the animals.

"She's an amazing equestrian," Kelli says, "so she taught me how to respect and ride horses. She owned a horse, too, so it was our special thing together to go take care of our 'babies' every day."

Kelli learned a great deal of responsibility at a young age from caring for her horse. She was entirely in charge of the care and welfare of her pet: feeding, watering, bathing, and exercising Jezebel, her first horse, along with cleaning the paddock.

"I always smelled a little bit 'horse poopy' at school," Kelli says. "It was embarrassing but worth it."

One of Kelli's joys was to spend many hours riding her beloved animal. There were beautiful trails in the area, so she and her friends would meet and go for long rides. She also rode her horse in local parades during every major holiday.

Kelli remembers Jezebel with fondness.

"She was an extremely gentle retired racehorse, and my best friend," Kelli says. "She would let me do anything with her. I could even take a nap on her back if I wanted. She and I had a very special bond. I loved her so much."

"He was so cool," Kelli says. "He had a lot of spirit and kept me on my toes."

As Kelli became a more experienced rider, her mother allowed her to start competing in local jumper horse shows, earning her fair share of ribbons.

"Having horses as a child was the best," Kelli says. "I learned so much from those majestic creatures. I credit owning and taking care of them as a child with how responsible I became as an adult, along with my love of all animals, big or small."

Jezebel lived to be an old horse. One day, Kelli's mom took the animal to an old-age pasture. When Kelli said goodbye to her beloved horse, she held Jezebel around the neck and sobbed. She'd had so many wonderful memories with that horse, and she'd been her friend for seven of the most important years of her life. Saying goodbye to her was one of the hardest things she ever did. But she knew that Jezebel would be happy living out the rest of her years on a beautiful pasture with nothing to do but eat and sleep. That was the only thing that gave her solace. Doing what was best for Jezebel gave her the strength to let go.

"I'll never forget Jezebel," she says. "I treasure every moment that I got to spend with my horses. They're forever in my heart and soul."

Kelli's mother continued to own, train, and care for horses all through Kelli's childhood. She still does to this day.

"Whenever I visit my mom in Northern California," Kelli says, "the first thing I do, after hugging her, is jump on one of her horses and go for a ride."

For most of her childhood, Kelli and her family lived in a suburban house with a large front yard and plenty of fruit trees. Kelli and her brothers would pick fruit right off the tree and eat it until their bellies hurt. Everyone in the neighborhood knew each other. The kids played outside, going from yard to yard. Kelli's parents left their front doors open, and neighborhood children came in and out all day long. It was a safe and friendly place, and everyone looked out for each other. The kids walked to and from school in a big group, talking and laughing.

Every year, the Storms family would rent a cabin at Mammoth Mountain, where they would spend a week camping, fishing, and hiking. There would be competitions on who could catch the biggest fish, along with cozy nights in front of the fireplace with board games and hot chocolate.

Every summer, the family would also visit Catalina Island, where Kelli's father's family grew up. Catalina Island is a quaint little community about an hour's boat ride from Los Angeles. There, Kelli and her brothers would spend time with their large extended family: grandparents, aunts, uncles, and cousins. The kids would run barefooted all over the island. They hiked, played army, and snorkeled. They enjoyed swimming, surfing, boating, and driving a golf cart around.

"Back then, no one cared if you were a child driving," Kelli says, "so we had a lot of fun piling a whole bunch of us kids into that golf cart and cruising down into town. Sometimes we would get all the way into town and realize we were missing a kid. They would have fallen off the side along the way, so we'd have to go back and get them. No children ever got hurt, and we all had a good laugh about it."

Besides the Storms' annual trips to Mammoth and Catalina Island with their Southern California relatives, there were summer mountain trips with their Northern California relatives for more camping, fishing, and hiking. Kelli's parents came from large families, so everything was always about family.

"When I think back on my childhood," Kelli says, "I have nothing but great memories. We were middle class and money was always tight, but we were happy."

Some of her favorite memories involved her brothers.

"They all had great senses of humor," Kelli says, "so we grew up playing practical jokes on one another or seeking out adventures."

Her brothers loved putting cellophane tape over the doorway and watching someone come through with their hands full and, as Kelli remembers, "totally eating it."

The boys also played that joke on their mother a few times when she brought home groceries. Their mom would end up on the floor surrounded by bread, fruit, and broken eggs. The Storms brothers would also be on the floor, consumed in belly laughs…and later cleaning up the mess they'd made. Mom laughed the first time. The second time wasn't funny anymore, and all the brothers learned what being on "restriction" felt like.

They boys enjoyed rigging cups of water above Kelli's bedroom door so that when she went into her room, the water would fall and drench her head and her clothing.

"We were always hiding somewhere to try and scare each other," she remembers. "We would use big moving boxes to hide in or build our forts."

When they would tire of their forts, they would flatten those same boxes and use them to race down the slick ice plant next to their home—a year-round California sledding adventure.

"We were so fearless," Kelli says, "and so competitive with one another. We were always trying to beat each other down the hill."

When their parents looked out the window, they would often see their petite daughter sitting on a flattened piece of cardboard, racing neck and neck with one of her brothers, screaming in delight as her blonde hair blew back in the wind. They would also see their youngest son, Kevin, sitting behind Kelli on the "sled" and hanging on for dear life.

"I wanted to beat my brother Bill so badly," Kelli says. "He was great at sledding and always a natural athlete in everything he did. When we were sledding, I would grab Kevin and throw him on the back with me for more weight and faster speed."

Bobby was five years younger than Kelli. He was energetic and kept the family on their toes.

"He was always on the go," Kelli says. "Cute as a bug." The family called him "Vanilla Flash" because of his energy and white-blond hair…and because he was, well, a little streaker.

"If you turned your back for one minute," Kelli remembers, "Bobby would be gone, off running down the road. All he would leave behind was a pile of clothes. He loved being naked. When he was about four years old, he took his clothes off in the middle of a department store and started running. Some people approached my parents and asked, 'Is that your naked child over there?' My parents just shrugged and said, 'Yep, that's Vanilla Flash!'"

Kevin was ten years younger than Kelli and always her "little baby," as she describes him.

"He was very smart, talented, and could get whatever he wanted whenever he wanted it," she says.

Everyone who met the little boy commented on his undeniably engaging personality. Even as a small child, he could win the hearts of anyone whom he came in contact with. Every time Kelli's mother would bring the children to the grocery store, Kevin somehow always ended up with a giant cookie in his hand. His brothers and sister would look at him and wonder how that happened.

"My mom would turn her back for one second," Kelli says, "and Kevin would have a cookie. It happened every single time."

One day, Kevin's siblings watched him in action to see how he was getting these cookies. They saw him walk up to the bakery counter and pull a forlorn face. Then he told the ladies who worked there that he hadn't had anything to eat all day and was so terribly hungry. The cashiers felt so sorry for him they gave him a giant cookie. One of the workers approached Kathy Storms.

"You should be ashamed of yourself," she said. "What kind of woman doesn't feed her child? He's starving!"

Kathy shook her head and said, "Honey, you've just been had by a five-year-old con artist!"

Needless to say, the jig was up. Kevin would have to find a new scam to get his free cookies.

"He was always up to something," Kelli says.

Dinnertime at the Storms house was always an adventure. Bob Sr. would tell his kids no horsing around at the dinner table, but that just made them want to do it more. While eating their food, Kelli and her brothers would try to make each other laugh when their father wasn't looking. Bill was the comedian of the family, and often the instigator.

"He could make us laugh just by looking at us," Kelli says.

Bill started the family trend of hiding food he didn't want in his siblings' milk, and soon Bobby and Kevin followed.

"Whenever I took a drink of milk," Kelli says, "I would find a big gulp of wet food. It was disgusting."

Despite all the humor at the dinner table, their father was strict about horseplay. While joking around, the kids kept their mouths clamped tightly shut so no giggles would escape. Suppressing their laughter while taking a drink would cause milk to squirt out their noses. Sometimes it was water or juice. All of this exasperated their father, who was just trying to enjoy a peaceful meal with his family after work.

One time, however, their dad got caught up in the antics and joined in on the laughter. It happened when all four kids had just snorted liquid out of their noses simultaneously from laughing so hard. Dad burst out laughing…so hard that a green bean shot from his nose! The sight of that long green bean shooting out of their strict father's nostril like a heat-seeking missile caused the kids to double over in belly laughs.

The teen years were also filled with adventure. When Kelli turned sixteen and got her driver's license, her parents gave her a 1976 Pinto. It was white with red and blue stripes, the colors of an American flag.

"It was completely embarrassing," Kelli says.

Her mother made Kelli take her brothers everywhere they needed to go, since she was the oldest and the only one who could drive.

"All of a sudden, I was their limo driver," Kelli says. "I was so irritated. Every time they tried to get in the car, I would step on the gas and make them run to get in. They would just barely get to the car and open the door, and I would step on the gas again and make them run. This would go on until my brothers would get so mad that they would start kicking the car. I would laugh so hard every time. That was my revenge for having to take my brothers to school. Between the four of us, we went to three different schools. It was quite a feat to get everyone to school on time, and then back to pick them up. Even though I have a really good relationship with my brothers now, we definitely had our sibling rivalry growing up."

One cause for family laughter came about when Kelli was in her late teens. She was getting ready to play in a softball game. She'd made the all-star team and was very proud of herself.

"I had a pretty big head about it," she says. She'd been primping in the bathroom for hours.

"Kelli, we're going to be late," her mom shouted. "You're taking too long."

"Okay, just a minute," Kelli said as she carefully curled her bangs with a hot curling iron so they would look good under her baseball cap. She was at an age where she was concerned about what boys thought, and there was going to be a cute boy at the field that day. She had a huge crush on him. She wanted to look good for this boy, even if he would probably never notice her beautifully curled bangs tucked under a softball cap with a long brim.

"I was so vain," Kelli says now, laughing. "I thought those bangs would make a difference in getting that boy or not. Here I was, about to play in my all-star game, but all I could think about was this boy and my hair. Teenagers and their priorities!"

Time ticked on as Kelli fussed in front of the mirror with her hair.

"We need to leave now," her mother said, "or you're going to miss your game!"

"Okay, okay." Kelli tried to hurry, but in her nervous haste, the curling iron slipped out of her hand.

*Owwww!*

"I actually burned my eyeball," Kelli says, shaking her head ruefully. "My *eyeball*!"

She was rushed straight to the emergency room.

Meanwhile, Kelli's dad, who was also her coach, was on the baseball field, pacing back and forth as he waited for her. This was before cell phones, so there was no way of getting a hold of anyone to find out where Kelli was. Little did Coach Dad know that his daughter was being treated in the emergency room for a burned eyeball.

"I didn't make the game, obviously," Kelli says, "but when we did arrive, I got a lot of attention and sympathy. Luckily, my dad couldn't be mad at me for being late."

Kathy Storms felt so sorry that Kelli had missed her all-star game that she took Kelli and her crush out for ice cream.

"The cute boy was looking at me from across the table with my big bandaged eye," Kelli says with a laugh. "I was wearing a giant black patch with white gauze poking out from underneath. So attractive. He asked how I hurt my eye. I said, 'When the curling iron slipped out of my hand, it burned my rectum.' The boy just stared at me. I continued on, saying, 'Don't look so worried. The doctor said it was just like skinning my knee; it's no big deal.'"

Kelli's mom nearly spat her food out when she heard her daughter say the word "rectum" instead of "retina." Her daughter had a habit of accidentally mixing up words sometimes, but never to that extent!

"I had no idea what I'd just said," Kelli says, "but the boy was looking at me like I'd just ripped my arm off. He looked mortified and stopped eating. In fact, he looked as though he was going to throw up. So I assured him that my rectum was going to be just fine, that it will form a scab and heal up just fine and blah, blah, blah… My mother jumped up and said, 'Kelli! Stop talking!' You did not burn your *rectum*! You burned your *retina*."

Kelli stared at her mother, and then the boy, aghast. *Oh my God, what did I just do?* She felt her face burn with embarrassment.

"I begged my mom to take me home," Kelli says. "Needless to say, I never saw that boy again…"

Kelli's high school years, while filled with fun, were also a time of responsibility and hard work. Besides caring for her horses, she looked after her brothers, had a heavy nightly load of homework, and worked at Fonzerelli's, her uncle's pizza joint. She dated a few boys, but didn't have time for a steady boyfriend.

"I was too busy," she says. "Working at the pizza place was my first taste of working hard and getting a paycheck. I loved it! I had the best time meeting new kids from other high schools and making pizzas."

After summer was over, Kelli worked at the local ski and skateboard shop on weekends. She was a skier and belonged to the ski club in high school, so working at a ski shop was a necessity for her. That allowed her to ski at a discount at the local mountains, and because that same ski shop had another store up in Mammoth Mountain, she got to ski there for a discount, too.

Kelli also loved tuning up the skateboards. At that time, it was unusual to see a female working on skateboards.

"There were two of us girls who tuned up the skateboards," Kelli says, "and we were badasses."

Then one day, during Kelli's junior year in high school, her parents decided to separate.

"It was a tough time for us," she says.

Her father moved out, and her mother started working nights as a waitress in Huntington Beach. They would take turns being with the kids. Kelli started taking on a more "mother-like role."

"As you can imagine," Kelli says, "helping take care of three rambunctious boys wasn't easy."

It was during that time that Kelli learned she had a knack for teaching, and had an empathetic side that enjoyed being with children.

"I realized I was very patient," Kelli says. "I really like and understand kids."

After high school, Kelli's parents got back together. Her father got a job transfer, and the family moved up to Northern California.

"It was a very cool place to live," Kelli remembers. "We were thirty minutes south of San Francisco, which was a lot of fun."

She started working at the racquetball/athletic club. She quickly learned to play racquetball, and loved it. She began participating in tournaments, and eventually toured for a summer as a professional racquetball player with her doubles partner. After two years, she had the opportunity to visit a friend on the island of Kauai, Hawaii, and packed up her things to go stay for two weeks.

She ended up staying for two years.

She moved to the island of Maui and immediately got a job at a restaurant on the beach called the Crab Catcher. The place also had a pool with a bar, and she worked around the pool as a pu-pu waitress. The management encouraged all of the employees to come up with nicknames for their nametags, so Kelli used her childhood nickname, Stormy. Pretty soon, everyone knew her as Stormy on the island of Maui.

During those years, she worked and played and dated. She was young and carefree. Life was good.

"I met people from all over the world," Kelli says. "I had the best time rooming together with friends, working, exploring, and living. I made new friends all the time, people who are still in my life to this day. I trusted people completely." She pauses, and a shadow passes across her face. "I loved that open and trusting side to myself. I never knew how much I valued it until it was later stolen from me by the Easters."

At that moment, though, back in Hawaii, "Stormy" was blissfully happy.

She was young and carefree.

Soon, she would move back to the mainland and meet a man who would forever change her life…

# four

On a crisp December night in Newport Beach in 1986, Kelli accepted a date with a guy she'd met through friends. Although she thought the guy was cute, she was getting more of a friend vibe from him. She suggested they meet some of their mutual friends for Taco Tuesday at El Torito Grille in Newport Beach. Kelli's date was visiting from out of state for the summer, so he was staying with his uncle. His uncle, coincidentally, was having a private wine tasting at a restaurant called Five Feet across from El Torito Grille.

Kelli and her date popped in to El Torito Grille to say hi to her friends, and then headed over to the other restaurant.

As they walked in, Kelli saw a group of men sitting at a long table. The table was covered with elegant place settings, platters of food, and many bottles of expensive wine. There was a separate glass on the table for every varietal of wine, which meant multitudes of shimmering glasses. The food looked mouthwatering.

"I was twenty-five-years old," Kelli says, "and even though I'd been to my share of expensive restaurants, I was blown away by what I saw. The chef, Michael Kang, was pairing his good food with amazing wine that my date's uncle and his friends had brought in. It all looked so enticing that I couldn't wait to sit down and join in."

As Kelli stared at the table in awe, a tall man caught her eye.

"He was so handsome," she says. "I was immediately drawn to him. Transfixed, captivated."

The man was Bill Peters. He wore a tailored black suit that fit his physique nicely. He had long red hair that was pulled back in a ponytail, and, as Kelli remembers, "a very cool goatee."

She couldn't take her eyes off the handsome man. "Never in my life had I looked at a man and thought to myself, 'He's exactly the kind of guy I want to marry,' but that's what I was thinking. I just couldn't stop staring at him. I was completely drawn to him."

Bill stood up to introduce himself.

"Hi," he said to Kelli, holding her hand and her gaze. "I'm Bill."

"I'm Kelli," she said, feeling a little giddy.

"You look familiar," he said.

Kelli had such a warm, comfortable feeling about him that she responded, "You look familiar to me, too." In fact, he did feel familiar, in that gut-knowing way that a woman has when she senses she has just met her soul mate.

Bill later said he felt it, too.

As Kelli looked into Bill's eyes, she was struck with a deep sense that she was going to be with this man for a very long time. They had an immediate connection that felt both real and right.

Kelli says, "This might sound crazy, but I knew Bill was the love of my life the minute I saw him. Not met him, *saw* him. How is that possible? I just knew. I'd been in lust plenty of times, but never had I looked at a man and thought, 'Marriage, kids, lifelong partner,' but something happened when I met Bill. It wasn't butterflies; it wasn't giddy; I didn't get flustered. It was something else. I felt at ease and comfortable with him, but it was more than that. He was completely irresistible to me."

Bill pulled out a chair and asked if she would like to sit down.

"I took a seat next to him," Kelli says, "and that's been my seat now for thirty years."

As for Kelli's date, she says, "If you're wondering about him, I wasn't so coldhearted as to leave him in the dust!"

Earlier, at El Torito Grille, she had noticed her date was having a very enthusiastic conversation with her girlfriend, Roseanne. Kelli was halfway through her conversation with Bill when she excused herself from the table. She ran across the street to Taco Tuesday and brought Roseanne back with her to the private wine tasting.

Kelli approached her date with Roseanne.

"I'm sorry for the last-minute switch," she said to him, "but I hope you'll understand. My girlfriend thinks you're hot, and you seemed interested, too. So if you don't mind, I'll leave you two to get to know each other better so I can continue my conversation with Bill over there."

"Sure," her date said. "I get it." He and Roseanne turned to each other and immediately became engrossed in conversation. Kelli went back over to Bill again with a skip in her step.

Kelli laughs now at the memory. "It all worked out. After all, I really didn't know that guy, and Roseanne was clearly more his type. They hit it off, and Bill and I got to enjoy the rest of our night together. It was a win-win for everyone."

That night, Bill walked Kelli to her car, which happened to be parked near his. Although they'd already talked all night, they didn't want to stop, so they continued their conversation. Bill told her he owned a restaurant and also sold wine. He worked at an eclectic wine company that only repped high-end varietals: unusual and specialized vintages that most people hadn't heard of.

She told Bill about herself, as well: how she loved animals and shared a condo with her mom in Dana Point.

"Does your mom like wine?" he asked.

"She loves it."

Bill went to his car and brought out a case of very fine wine, along with another case of expensive champagne. "Give these to your mom for me," he said.

Kelli's heart flooded with warmth. Who was this guy? He was so open, generous of himself, and kind...plus very sexy. He was exactly what she wanted in a man.

Bill smiled at her in a way that gave her a happy feeling in her stomach. "Would you like to go out sometime?"

"Sure," she replied.

"Would you do the honor of accompanying me to my Christmas party at my restaurant?"

"Yes," Kelli said. "I would love that."

"Then it's a date."

Later that evening, when Kelli gave her mom the wine and champagne, her mom said, "I have a very good feeling about this one, Kelli."

"So do I, Mom," Kelli replied. "So do I..."

As Kelli got ready for her first date with Bill, she kept thinking about how he made her feel. There was something so different about him. He gave her such a good feeling inside, much different than the proverbial butterflies—or knots—with some of the men she had dated.

"Before Bill, I couldn't truly relax around any of the guys I went out with," Kelli says. "It was as if I was trying to make something work that didn't feel quite right."

Indeed, Bill Peters gave her an excited feeling in the pit of her stomach...but the right kind.

Kelli felt beautiful that night of their first date. Since it was a semi-formal affair, she wore a floor-length fitted black dress. Her long blonde hair was wild and curly, making her feel like a sexy lioness.

When Bill showed up at her door, she became instantly tongue-tied. He was so gorgeous! He wore a tailored Hugo Boss tuxedo, and his red hair was in a neat ponytail. She loved his goatee, which gave him a slightly renegade look, something she'd always loved since her father was in a band.

"Bill was so handsome," Kelli says. "He just did it for me in every way."

At the party, they talked and laughed and ate. They didn't dance, though, because of Kelli's two left feet despite having taken dance lessons as a girl. But it was fine…they were close, anyway. Bill never left her side. His hand was always on her back, and he made her feel special.

There were women there, of course, who also couldn't take their eyes off Bill. They flocked around him, flirting and tossing their hair and trying to get his attention. After all, he was tall and handsome and owned the restaurant, The Crown House, where they worked. While Kelli felt a momentary pinch of jealousy, she could also see that Bill wasn't really into any of the women who crowded around him, giggling and flirting.

But Bill seemed to have eyes for only one woman: Kelli. He made her feel secure by being attentive. While he enjoyed the female attention, he didn't seem like a player. Something in Kelli just knew that they would be together always…that he was "the one."

"We were a couple right away after that," Kelli says. "And it was perfect."

They dated exclusively from then on, and days blended into months and then years.

"We were just always together," Kelli says.

Bill often took her on business trips with him. They would also travel for fun, heading off on mini-excursions almost every weekend. They would go to the Ritz-Carlton in Dana Point, or hole up in a romantic inn in Santa Barbara, or hide away in a villa in Napa.

Their times at home were equally romantic. They made dinners together and spent hours cozied up in bed, talking about their dreams for the future and their life together.

Bill introduced Kelli to blues music. He'd been an amateur photographer at one point, and showed her pictures of the famous musicians he'd met when he'd gone to their concerts: Jimi Hendrix, Janis Joplin, Rod Stewart, along with such blues greats as Albert King, Muddy Waters, Freddie King, and Junior Watson. Bill himself was a musician who played guitar and harmonica.

"I was mesmerized whenever he played," Kelli says. "He's talented in so many different areas—a true renaissance man."

Of course, the women who flirted with Bill were still there on the periphery, always reminding Kelli that she'd won the prize over hungry rivals.

"It did cause me some insecurity sometimes," Kelli says. "When we'd go to a restaurant, inevitably he always knew someone. A girl he dated might wait on us. Or another might come up and gush all over him and act like I wasn't sitting right there. Bill enjoyed having a lot of female friends, and they enjoyed him, too. It wasn't always easy, and I made sure to never give him crap about all that female attention, but it still hurt sometimes. But that's the price a woman has to pay when she's with such a good-looking and charismatic man."

One night, Bill called her with an odd sound in his voice.

"Is there anything wrong?" Kelli asked.

"No, not at all. Why would you say that?" he replied.

"I don't know, you just sound different."

"Everything's fine." His voice sounded strained. Kelli read it as guilt.

Just then, she heard a female voice in the background say, "Do you want me to leave?"

Kelli's heart dropped to the floor. "Who's that?"

"Just a friend," Bill said, but his voice sounded so strange that

Kelli knew the woman wasn't just a friend. Her worst fears had come true. Yes, he'd telephoned her out of guilt (albeit with the woman right there), but that didn't change anything.

It appeared that he'd betrayed her after three years together.

"How could you?" Kelli asked as tears welled up in her eyes. Before he could answer, she told him it was over and hung up.

She cried all night long, deep sobs racking her shoulders and her face buried deeply in her pillow.

In the morning, she was startled to see that her pillow had the perfect outline of her face embedded in it. Her eye makeup and lipstick and blush had all smeared from tears into the exact outline of her face: a perfect painting of grief.

Kelli took the pillowcase and hung it up so it would serve as a daily reminder to her what had happened. She wanted that pillowcase to keep her strong so she would never cave and go back to Bill after what he'd done.

He called her repeatedly after that, and came by, but she refused to take his calls or see him. She'd given her all to him, been a devoted girlfriend of three years, and loved him with all of her heart…and he'd cavalierly betrayed her with another woman. He was not the man she could spend the rest of her life with after all.

Kelli tried to move on with her life. It wasn't easy. Bill was always on her mind, and memories of their three years together kept replaying themselves through her mind in a painful, tear-inducing loop. She would let herself cry, but then she would take a deep breath and square her shoulders and force herself to be strong. She didn't want a man who wasn't one hundred percent in love with her. And if he'd gone and been with another woman, he couldn't possibly love her.

She knew one thing for sure, though: she would never forget the fun-loving, long-haired man who'd swept her off her feet and shown her true love for the first time in her life. For that, she would always be grateful. She would never regret having met Bill Peters.

Nine months later, Kelli was in a video store looking for a movie to bring to her mom's house. It was Christmas time, and she thought it would be fun to watch a lighthearted movie, maybe a comedy, with all the extended family.

She rounded the corner and ran smack into Bill.

"Kelli," he said in the most broken voice she'd ever heard. He gazed into her eyes with such pain, such longing, that she felt a rush of emotion—all those feelings she'd tried to bury for nine months came flooding back all at once.

They talked—she doesn't remember about what—but all she could think about was how handsome he looked. He looked at her with tenderness in his eyes, and it was then that she knew he'd never gotten over her.

They made small talk for a while longer, and then he asked what she was doing for Christmas.

"I'm going to my mom's," she said. "What about you?"

"I'm working at my restaurant until nine," he said, still gazing at her with those soulful eyes.

Kelli met his eyes, and her heart turned over, as it always did whenever she was around him. She then did the unthinkable.

"Would you like to come over to my mom's for Christmas dinner?" she asked.

His face lit up. "Yes!" His reply was swift and immediate.

Kelli was surprised by not only his enthusiastic reaction, but by herself. She'd just invited her ex-boyfriend over for Christmas dinner on the spur of the moment! Why did she do that when she was still trying to figure out how she felt about him?

"I couldn't believe I did that," Kelli says, "but he looked so broken. Besides, it just felt right. Seeing him brought it all back, all the memories we had. It was as if no time had passed between us."

Kelli didn't know if Bill would show up at her mom's house, but she wasn't holding her breath. She'd moved on, for the most part, and wasn't going to sit around waiting for him. If he showed up, great. But if he didn't, her life would go on as it had. Their lives would take different paths. In time, they would both just be a memory of past love that would fade with years.

A short while later, there was a knock on the door. Kelli's mom asked, "Are you expecting anyone?"

"Maybe," Kelli said, her heart beating hard in her chest. *Could it be? Is he here?*

Sure enough, Bill Peters stood in the doorway with a big grin, holding four bottles of fine wine. Kelli and her family welcomed him in, and as they say, the rest was history...

From then on, Kelli and Bill's courtship was smooth sailing.

"His female groupies eventually faded out, and I never worried again," Kelli says. "He was fully committed to me, and me to him. It was wonderful."

They both worked a lot during that time. Bill owned the restaurant and traveled extensively for his wine sales job.

Kelli worked for a loan broker and a graphic designer.

Their weekends were spent relaxing together, going out to dinner or cooking for each other.

"Bill lived in a beautiful house in Laguna Beach," Kelli says. "He loved to cook for me. We would walk to the store and buy whatever was fresh and looked good. Then he would whip up a delicious meal that he would pair with really good wine. We just loved spending all of our time together."

Bill was revered by his peers as a wine connoisseur, and his eyes would light up whenever he would talk about it. He gave seminars, and Kelli would accompany him to tastings and events all over the country.

"He was so sexy when he would talk about wine," she says. "I couldn't take my eyes off him. He always knew everybody. It didn't matter what city we were in, what state—he could open up a conversation with a restaurant owner or a shop owner, and they would immediately know who he was from that moment on. We got the royal treatment wherever we went. Bill would take me shopping and pick out amazing clothes. He had incredible taste and always wore the best clothes himself. By day he surfed; by night he wined and dined me."

Kelli had always been a music lover, and that was something she also shared with Bill. "We loved going to concerts. That's always been my thing, and same with him. We had such an incredible connection."

Regular life was as enchanting as their travels. On most mornings, Bill would get up at six a.m. to surf before work, and Kelli would go down to the beach to watch him. She helped him zip up his wetsuit, and off he would go into the wild ocean to tear up the waves. Kelli sat on the beach, bundled up in a warm blanket, knitting scarves for her family and friends while she watched her man.

"Our life together was a dream come true," Kelli says. "Here I'd landed this guy who was wildly handsome, mature, sweet, established, and one of the best parts: a surfer!"

The beach also gave her a deep sense of calm.

"I'm so at peace there," Kelli says. "I would just sit on the sand and daydream about our future together. There was something so special about being out in nature, watching my boyfriend doing what he loved. He would come out of the water all salty and sandy and give me a big hug. We would kiss with the waves crashing in the background and the early morning sun warming our shoulders. It was a magical time. Going down to the beach to watch Bill surf every morning is one of my very favorite memories of our courtship."

After surfing, they would both head off to their respective jobs.

Soon, they moved in together. Kelli started to have maternal yearnings. They decided to get a dog and adopted a cute Corgi.

As Kelli tells it, "Corgis are big dogs in small bodies. That way, Bill got the big dog he wanted, and I got the little dog I wanted. It was a great compromise for us, something that Bill and I have always done well. He has the patience and tolerance of a saint, and I'm an energetic bundle of ideas, always on the go. We're the perfect balance to each other."

They named their dog Little Walter after one of Bill's favorite blues musicians. About a month later, the Corgi rescue center called, saying they had Walter's brother, who needed a home. Kelli and Bill couldn't say no, so they adopted another Corgi, whom they named Professor Higgins. They had both dogs for the next seventeen years.

"They were our first children together," Kelli says with a smile.

At that time, their neighbors also became their best friends.

"Every time Bill had a business trip to the wine country," Kelli says, "we would ask Eric and Grace to go along with us. We did this a lot. Neither of us had human kids yet, so we had a lot of freedom back then. We took a lot of trips to Napa, San Francisco, Las Vegas, you name it. We loved to eat at the finest restaurants and drink the best wine. We dated ten years before we tied the knot, and it was a whirlwind of joy and fun. He introduced me to so many things. He taught me about wine pairing with different foods, something I'd never known. I thought I was pretty worldly before I met Bill, since I'd already lived in NY, Hawaii, and California. At age twenty-five, I'd seen and done a lot of things. I was very independent and not looking for love when I found him. I was happy with my life. I lived on the beach, had a pretty good job, had my own thing going on. Bill really completed me on so many levels. That sounds so cliché, but I had no idea how incomplete I was until I met Bill."

Bill's restaurant, The Crown House, thrived during the early years of their courtship. It was situated in balmy, picturesque Dana Point right off Pacific Coast Highway. It was a popular restaurant that everyone knew about, famous for its food and music. It had an old-style feel, with red velvet couches and a dark, sultry bar. There were large, beautiful fish tanks all around the room with exotic fish gliding around inside. The room smelled of gourmet food, fine wine, and expensive perfume.

Kelli would stop there every night after work and have dinner while Bill was working. She loved talking to all the regulars and hearing their stories. It wasn't uncommon to see Kelli at a table, talking and laughing animatedly with new friends or bopping her head in time to the music. Bill would run over in between his restaurant duties and give her a kiss.

The entertainment was the highlight of the place. The musicians were people who had been around for a while, such as George Butts, a talented man who not only sang beautiful, slow, bluesy ballads, but wooed the ladies with his sexy jazz saxophone. The Crown House was a locals' hangout as well as a place that people visited from miles around.

Bill's father, Bill Sr., was also the chef at the restaurant. He'd started his career as a sous chef at Musso & Frank in Beverly Hills. After working many years in the restaurant business, Bill Sr. finally decided to open his own place. His first restaurant was a co-ownership of a place that is now called Delaney's. Then he went on to own The Crown Point, the Ivey House in Laguna Beach, the Bayshore House in Mission Viejo, and finally, The Crown House in Dana Point.

"Bill Sr. was such a special man," Kelli says. "He and I had the same birthday, and we had an amazing connection from the start. I loved this man more than anything. I wish he was still here. He was a grandpa to Sydnie for only one and a half years."

Bill Sr.'s wife, Jeanne, also helped run the restaurant.

"She was the hostess with the mostest," Kelli says. "She sang, she danced; she greeted everybody; she was the life of the party. Everyone loved her. She helped make that restaurant what it was."

Bill Jr. worked hard in his father and Jeanne's restaurant, which would eventually become his own. He spent long hours at the establishment and took pride in his job.

One day, though, tragedy befell their beloved restaurant and changed their livelihood forever.

Upon closing, one of the employees emptied a smoldering ashtray into a trash can, and it caught on fire.

At four a.m, Kelli and Bill got a call that The Crown House was in flames. They rushed to the restaurant, only to watch it burn to the ground in front of them. They held each other and cried. For Bill, who had worked at that restaurant ever since he was a child, it was a life-changing moment.

Animal-loving Kelli sobbed the hardest about the fish that had died in their tanks.

"I cried over those fish more than anything," she says. "Even though the restaurant was our livelihood, all I could think about were those poor, suffering fish."

Unfortunately, the insurance wouldn't pay out until years later.

"It changed everything for us financially after that," Kelli says. "We weren't ever able to rebuild after the fire."

No one ever pointed a finger at who had burned the restaurant down, and no accusations were ever made.

"It was an honest accident," Kelli says. "But it was devastating to all the families who worked there. Bill Sr. spent every last dime of his own money to keep the paychecks going for all the employees as long as he could. He didn't want to leave them stranded."

The Crown House was no more.

Kelli says, "A famous actor named James Cagney owned the land that the restaurant was built on, and when he died, he left it to his niece. After the fire, she didn't want to rebuild The Crown House. She wanted something more modern, so that's why the Salt Creek Grille is there now. It really was a blow to us all."

Bill Sr. was too old to start a new restaurant, and Bill Jr. was burned out from the restaurant business. Bill Sr. and Jeanne retired, and Bill Jr. decided to focus on selling wine instead.

---

**Bill** Peters proposed to Kelli Storms on a warm summer day in 1996.

"He got me a giant engagement ring," Kelli says, "but I was shy about it. I was afraid to tell him that it was too big and ostentatious." Kelli had never been one for showy things. A huge, glittering diamond, while something that most Orange County women might covet, just didn't fit Kelli's style or personality.

"It just seemed so frivolous," Kelli says, "and besides, we couldn't really afford it. I just wanted a simple symbol of Bill's and my love for each other."

She took the ring to have it sized, but the jeweler said he couldn't size it because the diamonds went all the way down the side and would pop out if it were made smaller.

"Unfortunately, you'll have to trade it in," the jeweler said with a look of regret, figuring it was her dream ring. Little did the man know that this was music to Kelli's ears. She hadn't wanted to hurt Bill's feelings, so this was the perfect excuse to get a simpler ring. She told Bill she had to trade it in, and he told her to get whatever she wanted.

Kelli chose a simpler ring that felt just right: a classic sapphire with diamonds around it—a smaller Princess Diana look.

At their twenty-year wedding anniversary, Bill surprised her with a new ring, this one just as simple and non-flashy as her first one.

"I treasure all the rings Bill has bought me," Kelli says. "For some reason, he loves getting them for me." She chuckles. "For example, he's a big fan of Comic-Con, so one year he got me a dragon ring. I never in my right mind would wear a dragon ring, but it was such a sweet gesture that I treasure that ring to this day. I've always appreciated Bill's attempts. I believe marriage is about compromise and appreciating the gestures that your partner does for you. It's about seeing the love in someone's actions. That's why Bill and I rarely argue to this day."

After Bill proposed, Kelli went into planning mode. They decided to have their wedding up in Lake Tahoe. On their way to the airport, Bill's best man, Eric, asked Bill for the wedding bands to hold until the ceremony.

Kelli and Bill looked at each other with wide eyes, and then burst out laughing. They'd forgotten to buy wedding bands! In the planning, they'd been caught up in their excitement about the wedding and had forgotten a most important detail.

They made a quick detour to Macy's for rings. Bill told Kelli to get anything she wanted, but true to form, she chose a plain gold wedding band. Bill did the same.

"We still wear those rings to this day," Kelli says. "All these years later."

Their wedding took place at the Cal Neva hotel in Lake Tahoe.

"It's a beautiful little old-time hotel on the lake," Kelli says. "There's a quaint chapel overlooking the water. It was quiet, perfect."

Kelli and Bill knew that it might be too long of a journey for many of their friends to make, since it was a plane ride away unless they were up for driving ten hours from Orange County. Kelli and Bill didn't want their friends and family to feel obligated to come if they couldn't afford the trip or take time off work.

"We knew it was a big expense," Kelli says, "plus it was far away. We told everyone that if they could find a way to get there, they're all invited. We would pay for the food and bar. We wanted to do more, but Bill's restaurant had just burned down, and we were strapped for money. We hoped some of our family and friends would be able to come, but we also knew it wouldn't be easy. You can imagine our surprise when every single person we invited came to our wedding. Every single one! Nobody missed it." She gets choked up at the memory. "People came from all over California, Arizona, New York, Texas, Nevada, Catalina Island, Oregon, you name it. It was so special to be able to share our wedding with the most important people in our lives. I still get emotional thinking about all those people who made the effort to share our important day."

The night before the wedding, Bill and Kelli had their bachelor and bachelorette parties, respectively. The guys gambled, watched the big fight between Oscar De La Hoya and Pernell Whitaker on a casino big screen, went to a strip joint, and just had a good old time. The girls taxied around to different casinos and nightclubs. They drank and laughed and watched live music.

The next day, at noon, Kelli and Bill got married on the lake.

During the wedding vows, Kelli got an unfortunate case of the giggles.

"The pastor said something about obeying me," Kelli says, "and Bill had to repeat it, and it just sounded so funny the way he said it. We'd been together for so long that our vows sounded almost comical. I started laughing and couldn't stop. At one point, my mom said, 'Kelli, stop laughing!' which only made me laugh harder. Then all of my bridesmaids started giggling, and then Bill joined in, and then my brothers, of course, and his groomsmen, and pretty soon everyone in the place was laughing. The pastor looked confused and asked, 'Why are you all laughing? Is my zipper down?' Of course, that made everyone bust up even more. It was a great moment."

The first dance was also an adventure. The wedding planner approached Kelli and Bill to ask which song they were using for their first dance. They looked at each other in confusion, and then burst out laughing once again.

"We need to pick a song?" Bill asked. He looked at Kelli. "What do you think? Which one should we use?"

They were under the gun so began quickly racking their brains.

"How about 'Love Will Keep Us Alive'?" Kelli suggested.

"By the Eagles?"

"Yes."

"Sure, what the heck?"

So "Love Will Keep Us Alive" it was, chosen minutes before their first dance.

There was one other problem: in all of their ten years together, they'd never danced one song together.

"The first and last time we ever danced together was at our wedding," Kelli says, laughing. "We were out there, awkwardly moving around the dance floor and trying to sway to the music. I could barely reach my arms up to him because he's six five and I'm five foot tall. My neck was craned up, and he was hunched over me. He looked down at me and said, 'I had no idea you were so short!' And I said, 'And I had no idea you were so tall.' We just laughed and laughed. One of my favorite photos is of that moment with the two of us on the dance floor, him so tall and me so short, and both of us just laughing so hard. It was truly the best moment of our wedding."

After their wedding, Kelli and Bill headed home to Southern California filled with the dreams and promise of starting a new life together.

"We didn't have a honeymoon," Kelli says. "We just went home and started our life together."

Their routine stayed much the same for the next years. They worked, cooked together, took long walks, went to the beach, and continued to spend every moment they could together.

"We just had an intense love," Kelli says, "which we have to this day. We can't be away from each other for too long. Our relationship has been tested, and we passed. We're still taking care of each other. Bill was so strong through all the turmoil the Easters caused us. I feel as though I don't really handle stress well, and Bill calms me, just like the first day we met. He's my hot tea, my fuzzy slippers, my warm blanket."

When asked who Kelli is to him, Bill says with a grin, "She's my toenail clipper, nose hair trimmer, and finger cracker. She's my hot mama."

During those early years of marriage, Kelli and Bill continued to frolic and laugh. Kelli was familiar with this after having grown up with her rowdy, fun-loving brothers.

One of the things Bill loved to do was grab Kelli, pick her up, and throw her over his shoulder. Because she was such an itty-bitty thing, this was easy to do.

Kelli recounts an incident at Fashion Island, an upscale outdoor mall in Newport Beach. Her friend, Lynn, was having lunch at one of the outdoor restaurants and heard a commotion nearby outside Saks Fifth Avenue. She looked over to see a tall man carrying a blonde woman upside down over his shoulder like a sack of potatoes. The woman was flailing her arms and legs and screaming, "Put me down!" The man just grinned and walked off with the woman kicking and screaming near his head as snooty onlookers gaped in astonishment.

Lynn shook her head and went back to her meal. "Typical Kelli and Bill."

Kelli says, "I said to Lynn, 'Why didn't you save me? I thought you were my friend. If it were me, I would have gone over and helped that poor girl. I wanted to be saved!'"

Lynn laughed and said, "No, you didn't."

Friends and family all noticed the fun that Kelli and Bill always had together and how they never seemed to get tired of each other.

The years passed. Life was good.

Soon, Kelli and Bill would welcome a new addition to their happy family.

# five

Having a family was something both Kelli and Bill wanted. After two years of marriage, even deeper feelings of maternal longing began to fill Kelli's heart. While she hoped for a pregnancy of her own, she'd been told by doctors that it wouldn't happen. So, in the year 2000, Kelli and Bill began the process of adopting a child. They were excited to welcome and raise a baby.

One day, Kelli went to lunch with her friend Sarah. She felt odd that day, as if something weren't right with her. She was nauseated, lightheaded, and just not herself.

When she turned down a margarita, Sarah asked, "Are you okay?" It wasn't like Kelli to turn down a margarita on a hot August Friday.

"I know this might sound dramatic," Kelli said to Sarah, "but I'm worried I might have cancer."

"What?" Sarah said. "Cancer?"

"I'm serious."

"Why would you say that?"

"I feel awful," Kelli said. "I just haven't been feeling like myself lately. Something's not right. I've been losing weight, feeling sick all the time, and everything smells and tastes bad." She clapped her hand over her mouth. "Oh my God, I'm so freaked out." She stared at

Sarah, her heart thumping with fear.

Sarah held her gaze with wide eyes. "Cancer? But you're so young, so healthy. You don't look like someone who has cancer."

"Maybe it's in the early stages. Gosh, I hope they can catch it early."

"You're really convinced it's cancer?"

"What else could it be? I've been feeling sicker and sicker every week, and it's not getting any better."

Sarah stared at her for a beat with an amused look on her face. "Stop for a second. I bet you're pregnant."

"Pregnant?" Kelli let out a short laugh. "That's not possible. The doctor told me I have a better chance of winning the lottery than getting pregnant."

"What are your symptoms again?"

"Nausea, weight loss, fatigue, night sweats, low energy, things smell bad and taste bad, and I just feel totally weird."

Sarah rolled her eyes. "You are so dramatic. You're not sick. You have all the signs of pregnancy."

"Or cancer."

"Wow, you're really looking on the bright side."

Kelli and Sarah exchanged an amused smile.

"Okay," Kelli said, "What should I do?"

"Go straight to the doctor. Call them and tell them you're coming. Pee in a cup and ask for a blood test. Call me when you get the results." Sarah paused and grinned. "By the way, I'm never wrong. I know you're pregnant. Also, you're having a girl. I can tell by the way you look."

"Um, okay, if you say so." Kelli laughed. "So according to you, I'm pregnant with a girl, even though the doctor says there's a better chance of a snowball surviving in hell."

"You'll see."

"Whatever. I'll call the doctor and go get a blood test to see what's wrong. But right now, I've gotta go home and rest. I feel like crap."

"Call me as soon as you know," Sarah said.

"I will."

Kelli and Sarah paid their bill, and then Kelli hugged her friend goodbye. As she made her way to the door, she heard Sarah call out after her, "You're pregnant, Kelli Peters!"

On her way home, Kelli called her family doctor and made an appointment. When the receptionist asked why she was coming in, Kelli explained her symptoms and said, "I think there's something really wrong with me. I think I need to be tested for cancer."

A few days later, she handed a vial of urine to the nurse. The doctor entered the room and said that she would order a blood test, since Kelli was so pale, sick looking, and had clearly lost weight. Kelli asked if bad smells and tastes were a sign of cancer.

"They could be," the doctor said.

As Kelli drove home after her doctor's visit, she became emotional. As tears welled up in her eyes, she wondered how she would break the news to her family that she had cancer. She didn't know if she had it for sure, of course, but how else could she explain all the strange symptoms? Despite what Sarah thought, Kelli knew there was no way she was pregnant. After all, she hadn't gotten pregnant all these years with Bill, and the doctor had told her that she couldn't carry a child. So what else could it be but something bad…very bad?

With a lump in her throat and fear twisting her stomach, Kelli walked in her front door to hear the phone ring. She raced over to the phone and picked it up with trembling hands, sure that it was going to be bad news from the doctor.

Sure enough, the doctor was on the phone. "I have some news for you, Kelli."

"What is it?" Kelli asked. Her throat was dry. She held her breath, waiting for the bad news that was sure to come.

"You're not dying."

Kelli gave a sigh of relief. "Are you sure?"

"Yes. But there's something else."

"What?"

"You're pregnant."

Kelli nearly dropped the phone in shock. "Are you kidding me?"

"No. I'm not kidding you. You're pregnant. You're not very far along, but most definitely pregnant."

"But…there's no way!" Kelli said, unable to contain the excitement in her voice.

"The test doesn't lie," the doctor replied. "Congratulations!"

Kelli hung up, and then let out a squeal of utter joy and disbelief. *I'm pregnant. Pregnant!* She did a happy little dance around the room. Then she started pacing back and forth, muttering to herself, "Oh my God, I'm pregnant. Omigod, omigod…"

She couldn't wait to call Bill. She picked up the phone and dialed him at the office.

He picked up. When he heard her voice, he said tersely, "Kelli, I can't talk right now. I'm in an important meeting."

"Oh, okay. I'm sorry." Kelli immediately felt bad for interrupting him. His job could be highly stressful at times. "I'll make it quick. Bill, I'm pregnant."

"Really? This is what you're calling me about?"

Kelli blinked. "Yes. I'm sorry for bothering you."

"That's fine, but I really need to go. This is an important meeting, Kelli."

"Okay, I get it. I'm sorry."

"I'll talk to you later." Bill hung up.

Kelli stared at the phone for a long moment, tears welling up in her eyes. *What the heck?* Hadn't Bill heard what she'd said? They were pregnant. They were going to have a baby! She started pacing back and forth again. *Omigod, omigod…*

Suddenly, the phone rang. Kelli picked up to hear Bill's elated voice on the other end.

"Kelli, I'm so sorry. It didn't register. Did you say what I thought you did?"

"Yes," Kelli said in a trembling voice. "I'm pregnant, Bill. We're going to have a baby!"

"I'm coming home right now!"

Kelli continued pacing as she waited for her husband. A short while later, he burst into the house and took her into his arms. They hugged for a long moment.

Bill pulled back to look at her, his eyes glistening with emotion. "I'm so happy. This is the most wonderful news in the world. I love you, Kelli."

"I love you, too." She looked into the eyes of the man she loved. She realized that at that moment, she was the happiest that she'd ever been in her life. They were going to have a baby!

Kelli wasn't superstitious about the pregnancy, and began telling everybody that she knew about the baby to come. Her family and friends were as excited and overjoyed as she and Bill were.

Kelli loved being pregnant. As she remembers, "My pregnancy was amazing. It was such a miracle for us. Every day was so special. I got sick for a few months in the beginning, but then it was so fun after that."

Women would come up to her and beg to touch her tummy. Kelli was never one to get annoyed. In fact, she couldn't blame them.

"There's something so cool and special about a pregnant mommy," she says. "I now find myself drawn to them more than ever, after I had my child. I just want to go up to a pregnant tummy and give the baby some words of wisdom. Mine are: 'Take care of your mommy.

You're the love of her life.'"

Kelli treasured the feeling of a new life growing inside her. Every time she looked in the mirror and saw herself, she had to pinch herself at the blessing she was experiencing. As her stomach grew rounder with every passing month, the pregnancy felt more and more real. She was going to be a mother!

Every night, Bill would play music to the baby inside Kelli's belly. He wanted to make sure that their baby listened to all the great blues players.

Kelli would read books to their unborn baby every night. Her favorite was Dr. Seuss.

"My heart hurt with happiness," Kelli says. "I'd never felt so much love."

During the first trimester, everything made her ill. She couldn't tolerate the smells of smoke, alcohol, or certain spices without feeling the need to vomit.

Her coworkers at the loan office where she worked were understanding of her morning sickness.

"We were like a family," Kelli says, something she would say again about her friends at Plaza Vista Elementary School. "They looked out for me."

Kelli's boss was especially tolerant. Often, she would be in his office for a business meeting and would suddenly say, "Excuse me," only to retch loudly into his trash can.

After that happened more than once, her boss finally said in a wry tone, "Um…do you think you could bring your own trash can to puke in next time?"

As the due date approached, Bill continued to go with Kelli to every appointment, as he had from the beginning. The excitement grew for their entire family. It was as if the energy was contagious, a shared high that everyone was in on. There was going to be new life! A new baby to love!

When the time came to choose names, Kelli and Bill asked all of their friends and family to write down the names they liked for babies, both boys and girls. Together, Kelli and Bill would read over the lists, crossing out some names and putting stars next to others. Kelli's first choice for a girl was Sydnie, after the sassy redhead from the TV show *Melrose Place*. Because Bill was a redhead, Kelli was convinced that their baby would have red hair.

They found out they were having a girl, so Sydnie it was...although she didn't turn out to be a redhead after all.

Soon, the due date arrived. Sydnie was supposed to be born May sixth, but on May first, 2000, she went breach (feet first). The doctor moved the date up for a C-section on May third. That felt like a sign to Kelli, as she was terrified of a natural birth and had prayed for a C-section. Now her daughter was making sure her mom's wishes were granted. Their connection was already there.

Kelli says, "Syd and I were already on the same wavelength. She took care of me, and I, in turn, would take care of her."

Sydnie Kay Peters was born on May third, 2000, at 1:38 p.m. She was five pounds and twenty-one inches long. She was a beautiful, thin, and extremely long baby.

Bill was in the delivery room and cut the umbilical cord. As Kelli remembers, "He nearly fainted, but he did it..."

Kelli looked down at her beautiful baby girl in her arms. Tears filled her eyes as she whispered, "You are my baby, and you will always be safe in my arms. Thank you, my sweet Sydnie, for making our family complete."

Sydnie was instantly attached to her mother.

"She was a cling-on from day one," Kelli remembers. "It was the best thing that ever happened in my life."

Sydnie was the first grandchild on both sides of the family. She had three sets of grandparents, four grandmothers, and plenty of aunts and uncles. The day she was born, Kelli's hospital room was packed with family and friends. Bill threw a wine and cheese party in their room, and the party spilled over into the hallways. Even the nurses joined in the festivities.

As Kelli recalls, "Bill was so proud! He just beamed with pride at Daddy's little girl."

All of their friends stopped by. Everyone dressed up as if it were a cocktail party. It was a big occasion for everyone. The Peters and Storms families had been anticipating this moment for years.

"It truly was a grand celebration," Kelli says.

Everyone fussed over the new baby.

"She was so perfect and gorgeous," Kelli says. "She looked like a little doll, with her perfectly round head and beautiful, red, pouty lips and giant green eyes. She loved having us kiss her. Her lips were like little pillow lips with suction. Kissing her was addictive. You couldn't just give her one. She was so good, too. We were letting each person hold her to take a picture, and you could see the pride in their eyes. Their pupils would get bigger as they held her. Every single person in that room was so happy and proud to have Sydnie in their life. It was as if she was theirs, and in fact, if you were there and you were a friend, you were automatically considered an aunt or uncle."

Kelli looked down at her baby, breathing in her scent. Little Syd smelled of baby powder, sweet baby breath, and baby hair. Kelli couldn't get enough. She would just breathe in her baby daughter constantly: big, deep breaths.

Soon, it was time to bring the new baby home. Kelli insisted on putting a baby bed extension next to their bed so they could have Syd sleep next to them.

Kelli laughs. "It was all fine and dandy until we discovered babies don't sleep through the night!"

Bill had to drag himself to work every morning with barely any sleep, and Kelli was so sleep deprived that each day was pure survival.

Kelli then moved into another room so Bill could get some sleep before work.

"I remember getting up at the same time as Bill every morning and looking like complete crap," Kelli says, "and he would be all perky and happy and well rested."

As she grew, Sydnie's personality began to develop. She was always laughing, always curious, and funny. Kelli and Bill would giggle constantly at her antics.

She did all the normal things babies did, and she did them right on schedule, except for one thing: she never crawled the way other babies did.

"She had this weird thing where she would crawl backwards but never forward," Kelli remembers.

Sydnie did this odd crawl for a while until eventually she got so frustrated with her lack of forward movement that, one day, she just got up and started walking.

"We were sitting around watching TV and laughing about Sydnie crawling backwards," Kelli says, "and she must've had it with us. She suddenly just pulled herself right up in front of me and started walking!"

Kelli stared at her child, unable to believe what she was seeing. Sydnie was still a baby, just barely nine months old. And she was *walking!* How could this be?

*Nooooo!*

Of course, once Sydnie got a taste of walking, there was no stopping her. She went from walking to running right away.

"It was crazy," Kelli says, "I couldn't believe my luck. I thought I had three more months with a semi-stationary baby…but it wasn't meant to be. Sydnie hit the ground running and never looked back. To say that Sydnie kept me on my toes is an understatement."

Syd wasn't happy in the stroller or the grocery cart anymore. She wanted to run and run and run…

Kelli would laugh and tell visitors, "Just let her do a few laps, and she'll eventually get tired and come over to say hi."

As Sydnie got older, she was one of those children who loved making friends wherever she went. Children loved being her friend as well.

As Kelli remembers, "Sydnie was the happiest child. Her smile was so huge. She was so friendly to everyone."

Whenever Sydnie saw a child alone in the grocery store, she would go up to him/her and take the child's hand. It was a common occurrence for Kelli to be leaning into a frozen food fridge or perusing a shelf, only to turn around and see Sydnie standing with a random child next to her.

"Mom," Syd would ask, "can my new friend come over to play?"

"Where did you get this child?" Kelli would say. And then a frantic mother would come running around the corner to claim her kid.

Soon, it was time for Sydnie to start preschool and for Kelli to go back to work.

Every day, Kelli would drop her daughter off at school and then head to the office. She spent her days on her BlackBerry, working on securing mortgage loans. She would do quotes all day long and visit brokers out in the field. But her heart was not in her job like it used to be. Instead, all she could think about was her little girl. She felt as though she were missing a limb.

"I had major separation anxiety," Kelli says. "I just missed her so much. We'd spent every day together since she was born, and now we were away from each other. She was only three, and it seemed so young to be without her mom."

Kelli began dropping by the preschool after calling on brokers. She would peek in on Sydnie to see how she was doing. Her daughter would be playing happily with her classmates with a big smile on her face, but that didn't matter. All Kelli wanted was to be with her best friend in the world.

"Sydnie is so social that she absolutely loved preschool," Kelli says. "It was truly my issue. I had to accept the fact that she was growing up, but it wasn't easy."

Often, Kelli would sit in the parking lot and cry. Her heart was not in her job any longer. It was in motherhood.

At night, Bill would ask her, "How was work today?"

"Fine," Kelli would reply.

"Really? What did you do?"

"Oh, I drove around making calls."

Bill would give her a look. "That's not what the preschool said."

"Oh?"

"They said you spent half the day there again."

This happened so often that finally Bill suggested they find another way to make things work. They went over the finances in detail. They figured out that if they watched every single penny, ate all meals at home, and tightened their belts, they could make it work on one income. It meant having a very frugal existence, but Kelli jumped at the opportunity.

"All I wanted to do was spend as much time with my daughter as possible," Kelli says. "The years go fast, and I knew I would never regret being at home with her."

Kelli began looking for fun, free things to do around Orange County. "Because money was so tight," she recalls, "we had to look for the free activities. Luckily, we live in such a nice place that it was easy to do."

Kelli would often take Syd to her favorite place, the beach. She would sit on a blanket and watch Sydnie frolic in the water or chase seagulls. They collected shells, built sand castles, looked for sand crabs, and chased each other up and down the beach under the clear blue sky.

They also visited the Santa Ana Zoo, the farmers' market, or headed down to Huntington Beach for the Tuesday night street fair with free music. When the Orange County Fair was in town, they would go there as well. They went to swap meets, parks, and zoos. Their friend was captain of a whale-watching boat, so Kelli and Sydnie spent many hours together out on the sea looking for whales.

Home was just as fun. Kelli loved playing with her daughter. They had tickle fights and played hide-and-go-seek. They played dolls and ponies. They danced in the living room together, and built forts. Every night before bed, Kelli spent hours each night reading books to her little girl.

Kelli's mom, Kathy, said, "I know why you had a baby, Kelli: so you could have someone to play with!"

There were other wonderful memories. When Syd was about five years old, she would ask her mom repeatedly when her birthday was. Her mom started joking, "Every day is your birthday, Syd."

One day, Sydnie took her mother up on it. She asked Kelli to make her a birthday cake, even though it wasn't her birthday.

"Sure," Kelli said, and she spent a few hours baking a cake. They put candles on it, sang, and Sydnie made a wish and blew the candles out. Then Syd put a candle on her mom's piece, sang happy birthday to Kelli, and she also made a wish and blew the candle out.

Then Bill came home from work, and Sydnie also cut him a piece of birthday cake. They sang happy birthday to Bill, and he also made a wish and blew the candle out. This became a weekly tradition in their household for a while.

Kelli often made the same wish when she blew out her candle: "I wish for my daughter to always be happy like this."

During those early years, all of Kelli's wishes did come true. Her daughter was happy, and that was all that mattered.

Soon, it was time for Sydnie to start kindergarten, which would be the beginning of Kelli's volunteering life.

"I'll never forget that first day," Kelli says. "It was completely emotional and traumatic. But not for Sydnie, no way! She couldn't wait to run into the classroom. I was the one who was a complete emotional wreck."

To the embarrassment of herself and others, Kelli wept loudly as her daughter raced off into the classroom.

"She literally dropped my hand and ran," Kelli remembers. "I thought for sure she would turn around and look back at me, but she didn't. I stood there crying. Then, after a few seconds, she ran back out and said, 'Oops, I forgot to kiss you goodbye, Mommy.' I just broke down after that. When Sydnie said she'd forgotten to kiss me, it meant to me that she'd remembered me."

That first day of pick-up, the parents hovered outside the school, waiting to get their children. The teacher came out to tell them how great the kindergartners were and how proud she was of them.

"They're such nice little people," she said, looking around at all the moms and dads standing there. "We have a big class this year. Would anyone be interested volunteering to help in my classroom?"

A few of the parents exchanged glances. Kelli's heart immediately leapt. This would be the perfect opportunity to spend time with Syd and help her learn!

The teacher met Kelli's eyes. "If you're interested, be in my classroom tomorrow bright and early." She smiled. "And be prepared to get messy."

For Kelli, it had been a long time since she'd set foot in a kindergarten classroom.

The next morning, she got dressed in clothes that could be ruined, then drove Syd over to Plaza Vista Elementary School.

There were other parent volunteers there as well. Immediately, Kelli felt a kinship with them, these women who were treading on new terrain with her. They were all new to this world—the world of public school and kindergarten. Kelli was both excited and nervous.

Soon, she found herself helping out in any capacity that she could.

"It was a beautiful experience," Kelli says. "I'd never been part of a classroom before, helping little kids. Not only was I able to be there to watch Sydnie learn, but I was able to facilitate it, too. She loved having me there. We were so close. Getting to know all of Syd's classmates, with their bright eyes and eager smiles, was magical. I was hooked!"

At that moment, in her daughter's class at Plaza Vista Elementary School, Kelli Peters caught the volunteering bug. Her volunteering career would bring her some of the greatest joy in her life.

It would also later bring Jill Easter into her life.

# six

In some ways, Kelli Peters was born to be a volunteer. Once she started helping in the kindergarten class, she never looked back. She passed out papers, took children to the bathroom, answered questions, showed the children how tie their shoes, and helped them write their ABCs.

"It was trial by fire," Kelli says. "Kindergarten had thirty kids that year, so Mrs. Jones, the teacher, really depended on us. The kids were so needy at that age. They cried for their moms, so I was always holding one or another and comforting them. When they weren't crying or asking to go to the bathroom, they were wiping boogers on the walls or running around like crazy monkeys. They just wanted to play all the time, and we had to balance that with trying to teach them something. I was constantly cleaning the classroom or chasing one of them down or soothing wounded feelings or tending to boo-boos. It was nonstop, organized chaos, but I loved it."

During that first year of volunteering at Plaza Vista, she would walk through the classroom every day to have little kids with eager faces and bright eyes run up to her and give her hugs. They clamored to tell her about their days, their pets, or their latest interests. She pulled them close and listened to them pour out their hearts. Her own heart filled to the brim to see all of these wonderful little human beings talking over each other to share their interests with Miss Kelli.

"I was just an ordinary person," Kelli says, "but they made me feel so special. I loved the feeling of helping children and being part of their learning processes and growing up. There was no better feeling than being part of their lives. I didn't care that I wasn't being paid. The reward was so much greater."

At the end of the year, Kelli had t-shirts made that said, "I Survived Volunteering in Mrs. Jones' Class." The parent volunteers wore them around school, garnering knowing smiles and laughter of fellow parents and staff. Everyone knew that if a mom survived volunteering in kindergarten, she could survive anything.

The following year, Kelli again volunteered in the classroom, this time for first grade. That was the year she was first asked to run for the PTA.

"I'd successfully survived being a volunteer in kindergarten," Kelli says, "and still showed up to volunteer in the classroom in first grade. Some parents had quit forever after the kindergarten year. Only the strong survived!" She laughs at the memory.

Kelli was not only shocked to be asked to run for the PTA, but surprised to hear herself say yes.

"I loved volunteering and always said yes to everything," she says. "If someone needed help with something, I said yes. If they needed a parent to bring food for a party, I said yes. If a teacher needed help in her classroom, I said yes. Then I was asked if I would be interested in running for secretary of the PTA…and I naturally said yes. But then I immediately second-guessed myself. I was concerned that I didn't have the experience. I didn't think I would win. In my mind, I thought they just needed people to run." She shakes her head at the memory. "Well, I had no idea that I was the only person running for the office of secretary. So guess what? I won."

Once Kelli won the seat, her already busy life ratcheted up.

Her job entailed being at every single board meeting and general

## "I'll Get You!"

meeting. She was responsible for taking notes and minutes. Every important thing that was said or decided had to be recorded by Kelli, typed up and presented at the next meeting, and made available to all the parents and faculty.

"It sounded way too important for me to handle," Kelli says. "I was such a kick-back person, just into hanging out with Sydnie and being the best mom I could. Being on the PTA board was never in the picture. But I said I would do it, and I did."

The new job involved a great deal of responsibility. Every time the board convened for a meeting, Kelli would look around at her hardworking fellow PTA members and be filled with tremendous admiration.

"I couldn't believe how much they did," Kelli says. "I was completely impressed."

Kelli quickly learned that the women on the PTA were patient and willing to help her.

"They were so accepting of anyone who wanted to help," Kelli says. "This wasn't the PTA you hear about. It wasn't cliquey or snobby. They were in such desperate need for volunteers. They just so badly wanted to have parents show up to meetings and give input. It was so difficult to get parents to come to the meetings. Everyone was so busy, so they—the parents—trusted us to make the decisions for the school and the kids. We took it very seriously."

The Plaza Vista PTA worked hard to raise funds and ensure that the money was used to the benefit of all the children.

"The PTA did so many wonderful things for the kids," Kelli says. "We became event planners, speakers, advocates, fundraisers, liaisons…it sounds so intense, but the parents who donated expected a lot from us, so we worked hard, every day!"

As if Kelli didn't have enough on her plate that first year, she and Bill also decided to sign Sydnie up for soccer, which led to more volunteering.

"We were so excited at the prospect of watching Sydnie play sports," Kelli says. "I'd played sports from an early age and loved it. I just knew Syd would love it, too, being the energetic kid she was."

Out on the field that first day of practice, Kelli and Sydnie found themselves part of a positive and involved group of parents. Everyone was eager to start the season…but there was one problem.

They didn't have a coach.

The two original coaches had backed out last minute, leaving a team with no one to lead them.

All of the parents looked around at each other and wondered what to do next.

"How are the girls going to play without a coach?" Kelli asked a beautiful blonde woman with sweet, mesmerizing eyes standing next to her. The woman's name was Dina.

"Hey, how about if we coach the team together?" Dina asked.

Kelli didn't miss a beat. "Sure!" she replied, even though she didn't know the first thing about coaching or leading a team. But she felt confident that this woman knew what she was doing, or she wouldn't have suggested coaching.

Kelli thought, *I'll be her co-coach and happily support her in any way I can. I'll learn the ropes from her.*

The trouble was, Dina was thinking the same thing.

Neither of them had ever coached a sports team in their lives!

Once they discovered this, they both immediately started laughing.

"Oh my God, what are we doing?" Kelli said.

She and Dina flew into a mild panic. They had to learn the soccer rules and how to coach, fast! After all, they'd just committed to coaching their daughters' team for an entire season. There was no backing out now. The parents and kids depended on them.

Over the next few weeks, Kelli and her new friend Dina bonded over a self-imposed crash course on coaching U7 AYSO soccer. They spent hours poring over rules and regulations. They took classes and got certified, and they picked every coach's brain they encountered.

During that time, the two women learned an interesting fact: they'd given birth to their baby girls, Sydnie and Destiny, on the same day, at the same hospital, with the same doctor, and on the same floor!

"It was one of those incredible coincidences in life," Kelli says. "It was an amazing bonding experience, and Dina and I have remained great friends to this day."

Dina says, "I remember Kelli the night I gave birth. She was the one with the big party of friends and family, all dressed up as if they were going to a fancy ball. Fifty people, spilling out into the halls, including the nurses, who were all enjoying themselves, too. I could hear them all laughing and talking and toasting…while I was trying to sleep. I remember thinking, *Sheesh, the least they could do is invite me to the party!* But then again, I was so sleep deprived from my baby's difficult birth that I wouldn't have been much fun. But yes, I remembered Kelli from that day. It's so cool that we were right next to each other on the most important day of our lives: the births of our daughters. Our friendship truly felt meant to be."

That season, Kelli and Dina did their best to coach their daughters' soccer team.

"We came in last place in the league," Kelli says, laughing. "But we had a blast doing it. So did the girls."

Sydnie, in fact, had enjoyed her season so much that she continued playing soccer every year thereafter until she discovered art.

Kelli continued to volunteer in her daughter's classroom every year after that, never skipping a day. She also continued to run for the PTA. As each year passed, Kelli learned more. The teachers and staff all came to know her and depend on her.

"They all loved her," remembers Monique, Kelli's friend. "She was so efficient and so good with the kids. The teachers really relied on her. So did the PTA. She became an integral part of the school in every way."

Kelli, for her part, enjoyed being part of a viable community of parents, volunteers, teachers, and administrators all working collectively to ensure the best possible educational environment for the children.

"It was an amazing team effort," she says. "And the kids really benefited."

Every year, the PTA would give out awards to volunteers who went above and beyond the call of duty and chaired a project on their own. Kelli began to rack up awards.

Kelli chaired Spirit Week and spent countless hours putting packets together and licking envelopes with the rest of the PTA members.

That year, in 2007, she received a certificate of appreciation for her work on the PTA. She also received an appreciation of spirit award for designing a t-shirt for the children to wear during Spirit Days: a turquoise and dark blue tie-dyed shirt with, of course, a peace sign on it.

Kelli went on to receive certificates of appreciation for every year thereafter: 2008, 2009, 2010, and 2011. She was also given the prestigious Volunteer of the Year award in 2011.

Kelli was also involved with the DARE (Drug Abuse Resistance Education) program at the school. The program was committed to educating children about the dangers of drugs. Kelli was good friends with the DARE officer, Officer Mendoza, and they shared a mutual respect.

One of the most meaningful instances of Kelli's volunteer career at Plaza Vista was during Teacher Appreciation Week. During that week, the Irvine Public School Foundation told parents that if they donated twenty dollars toward the afterschool program in a teacher's name, that teacher would receive a certificate of appreciation. Parents could take it a step further and write something nice about the teachers they appreciated.

The first time a parent donated in Kelli's name, she cried. The note was from a stay-at-home father, Robert Passananti, and his wife, Hardip. Robert was dying of cancer but still had taken the time to acknowledge Kelli. The note that accompanied the certificate of appreciation said, *Thank you for being so great with the kids. You are truly one of a kind. Love, the Passananti Family.*

For Kelli, it was a profoundly moving experience.

"I wasn't even a paid teacher or staff member," she says. "I was just a volunteer parent putting in my time for free because I loved helping kids. Technically, I wasn't supposed to get these awards because I wasn't a teacher. And yet these parents had taken the time to not only donate in my name, but also write lovely words of appreciation about what I did for their children. It moved me beyond words."

Beverly, a school administrator, said to Kelli, "That's very unusual, but not at all surprising. Even though you're not a paid staff teacher, you're in the position to positively influence children's lives, and you do."

Every year, Kelli would continue to receive these certificates from parents during Teacher Appreciation Week. And each and every time, she was so touched that she would cry.

"They made me feel so appreciated," Kelli says. "It was then that I began to toy with the idea of becoming a teacher someday."

Unfortunately, Jill Easter came along and changed all of that.

# seven

The afterschool program (ACE) where Kelli volunteered at Plaza Vista Elementary School started at 1:30 p.m. every day. The program offered classes in cooking, clay, golf, tennis, volleyball, basketball, and art. At any given time, there were fifty or more children enrolled, with parent volunteers and teachers watching the kids. There was also the child development aftercare class, with kids constantly playing outside. The school was mostly fenced in, so children were never in danger or alone at any time. Kids also would stay after and play outside on the playground after the enrichment classes ended.

As a volunteer, Kelli would supervise the ACE program for the entire two hours of class time. She would go to each classroom and make sure all child and parent needs were taken care of. Sometimes, a child might have a nosebleed that needed attending. There might be a child vomiting in the clay class, or a bee sting in tennis, or a scraped knee on the playground. No matter what happened, Kelli was there to assist or help. Much of her time was spent escorting the younger kids to and from the bathroom. The coaches and teachers all had her personal cell phone number and email address in case they needed to reach her. She was the on-call person, always running from one classroom to the next.

"It was an adrenaline rush," Kelli says. "It was the place where I was happiest. I was near my daughter, I was around children, and I felt of service."

Five minutes before classes ended, Kelli would go to each of the outdoor classes and the sports programs and gather the children to line up for pickup. She would make sure the children had their water bottles, lunch bags, art projects, and schoolwork. She'd check for jackets and hats. As in most schools and aftercare programs, parents would arrive, and their children would go to them. That way, all parents and children were matched up and accounted for. There was no formal sign-out procedure for the afterschool program at Plaza Vista Elementary School (that has since changed). After all, it was considered a safe, enclosed program, and there had never been an incident.

Before the parents enrolled their children in the afterschool program, they each had to sign a page of rules published by the school that stated that all parents had to be there on time to pick up their children. They signed an agreement stating that if there was ever a delay in picking up their children, they would immediately contact Kelli, the head volunteer, or the program director through their personal cell phones or email addresses.

The ACE program had a policy that for every minute that a parent was late, he/she would have to pay a dollar.

"I could have enforced that," Kelli says, "but I never did." Instead, she would wait for late parents, sometimes up to an hour of her own time.

"I understood that they had busy, stressful lives," she says. "Plus, I loved being with the kids."

The parents were also responsible for making sure their children knew to line up and be ready for pickup. As children do, though, some would stay behind because they didn't want to leave their activities. Others would dawdle and take their time. Still others stayed behind because they enjoyed helping the teachers. Or sometimes parents would pick up their children in the back of the playground in order to walk home with them, so they told their children not to line up in front.

Kelli says, "For those parents who lived behind the school or wanted to walk home with their children, it was inconvenient to walk all the way around to the front of the school and wait when they could just get their kids from the back. That was actually against school rules, but no one enforced it. We had a very relaxed system, which has since changed, too."

One of those children who didn't like to line up was a sweet little blond boy named Layton (name changed to protect the child). He often liked to stay back and help his teachers. He was a likable kid whom the other kids and teachers enjoyed.

As Kelli describes him: "He was the neatest little boy. Sweet, helpful, just really cool in every way. We had such a great relationship. He loved to help. He was gregarious and friendly and never any trouble. One of the nicest little kids I've ever met."

On the afternoon of February 17, 2010, Layton didn't line up. To this day, no one knows why he stayed behind, but Kelli felt he was probably helping his teacher clean up, as was typical of him.

Kelli helped the kids get to the lineup area, the children were all matched with their moms and dads, and they all went home. There were no children or parents left over.

It was another successful day at the ACE program.

All seemed good.

Kelli went about the rest of her day.

She and Sydnie always enjoyed a fun little routine after lineup. Mother and daughter would go over to the cooking program because that class was an hour and a half long and ran later than the rest of the other classes. This was an opportunity for Kelli and Syd to nibble on something after a long day and spend some time together.

## "I'll Get You!"

The kids in the cooking class were always so excited to show off their culinary skills. When they saw Kelli, they would run up to her, jabbering excitedly about the newest meal they'd just cooked. Kelli would delightedly sample their cooking while the children watched her every bite. They would stare at her with huge grins on their faces, waiting with shining eyes for her reaction. As Kelli prepared to take a bite, the teachers would exchange amused, knowing glances.

"Even if the food wasn't good," Kelli said, "I always faked delight because I didn't want to hurt the kids' feelings."

She would take a bite and exclaim how great it tasted. She raved over the food and pretended to love every bite, even if sometimes it had an "interesting flavor," since it was made by seven-year-olds who sometimes put in a "dash of this and a pinch of that" when the teacher wasn't looking.

"I loved that those sweet little kids were so excited to share their creations with us," Kelli says. "They worked so hard to get it right. Surprisingly, most of their meals were very good. It was my and Syd's favorite time of the day."

On this particular day, the kids had prepared Chinese chicken salad and fried noodles with sesame dressing. Since Kelli didn't eat chicken, she gave her meat to Sydnie, who scarfed it down. The meal was delicious, and Kelli and Syd complimented the kids on their fine work and gave them lots of accolades. The children beamed with pride, watching with joy as Kelli and Syd not only devoured their own servings but asked for more.

"Those kids were learning how to cook some pretty gourmet meals," she says.

The dishes were also served with cornbread that the children had made from scratch. They'd made it with cornmeal, milk, and eggs, stirring it carefully with little hands and putting it into a preheated oven to bake until it came out with a lightly browned crust.

Kelli and Sydnie each had a few pieces of the cornbread topped with butter and honey. The kids crowded around their table, chattering in excitement.

Amidst it all, Kelli looked over at her ten-year-old daughter, sitting beside her with long brown hair and soulful green eyes. Syd was contentedly munching on her cornbread. She looked happy and peaceful. Syd exchanged a smile with her mom, and Kelli's heart flooded with warmth and love. She felt a rush of immense gratitude at that moment for the gift of such a wonderful daughter and life. Things seemed so perfect at that moment.

"I had finally figured out where I fit in life," Kelli says. "I was a mom, I was going to make a career somehow out of working with kids, and I was happy. No more difficult bosses. No more working for companies who set people up to fail. I was going to work with kids—pure, innocent children. I would walk into the school every day and was rewarded with hugs and laughter and beaming eyes from little children so proud of their artwork, cooking, and accomplishments. They thanked me for all my hard work with their hugs and love. Things were going so great."

The door to the culinary class opened, and Janice, an administrator, walked in. She immediately approached Kelli.

"Kelli," she said. "One of the moms is here to see you."

"Sure," Kelli said, and got up from her chair. This wasn't an unusual occurrence. Moms would often stop by to thank Kelli for looking after their children, or to bring her small gifts, or to ask questions about the ACE program and get help in signing up for classes. Kelli was used to interacting with parents, and enjoyed it. She'd never had anything but a positive interaction with any of them.

Sydnie followed Kelli outside. There was a woman standing by the front doors to the school wearing a long, flowing lounge dress. She had bleached-blonde hair and looked to be the high-maintenance type. There was something off about her, though: her hair was disheveled and sweaty, which looked out of place on her well-coiffed appearance.

Kelli says, "She looked like she was hiding something. Where had she been?"

Jill was a pretty woman, but her good looks were minimized by what Kelli describes as a "godlike attitude."

Jill was pacing in the hallway, near the front door. Next to her stood Layton, her son. His countenance was the same as always, which was fairly low-key and placid.

"He wasn't crying or upset in any way," Kelli says. "It would have alarmed me if he was. I don't like seeing any of the kids upset. But Layton seemed fine."

Jill, on the other hand, seemed agitated. She approached Kelli in a rush, her eyes wild and darting. "My two other kids are in the car, so I need to make this quick. Do you know why my son Layton didn't make it in the back door with the rest of the kids?"

"I actually don't," Kelli said. "Did you pick him up at the back of the building?" She asked this question since some parents picked up their children in that location.

"No," Jill said. "He came up with the tennis coach."

"Oh, good," Kelli said. "Sometimes kids like to stay back and help or clean up. Maybe Layton did that?" She turned to Layton and said, "Remember, your friend Hannah does that?"

Layton nodded. He looked confused. He tugged on his mother's arm. "Can we go, Mom?"

Jill kept her eyes trained on Kelli. "That's fine," she said. "No problem. I'm not accusing you of anything. I just wanted to know what happened."

"Sure, I understand," Kelli said.

Jill seemed satisfied with Kelli's answers. After she left, Kelli thought she seemed fairly reasonable, just an ordinary concerned parent.

Kelli and Syd headed back to the cooking class.

Kelli had just started eating her food again when Janice reappeared.

"Sorry to bother you, Kelli, but that parent is back and needs to see you."

"Sure thing," Kelli said, and got up and went out into the hallway again. Jill was waiting for her again with Layton. Her countenance was slightly agitated.

"I'm having a problem with why Layton was brought up by the tennis coach," Jill said.

"Well, he took a tennis lesson," Kelli said. "It happens sometimes if a child is slow to line up and the parents are waiting. If any of the coaches or teachers sees a child hanging back, they'll escort him or her up. It takes a village, and we all help out."

"He was crying."

"He was? I didn't know that." Kelli was perplexed by this statement. Layton had seemed fine when Kelli had seen him.

"Yes," Jill said. "He was crying." Her eyes bored into Kelli's. "He was standing outside crying for twenty minutes."

"That's impossible," Kelli said. She did a swift calculation. "Mrs. Easter, class ends at 2:30. I waited by the door until 2:35. You arrived at 2:40. The tennis coach had to leave by 2:40 at the latest to get to his next class, which starts at 2:45. So the coach must've walked Layton up at the same time that you arrived. In that ten minutes before you came, I'm sure Layton was either playing with the other kids out back or helping a teacher like he normally does. Did you ask him what he was doing?"

"He should have been already here waiting for me," Jill snapped.

"We give the kids five minutes to line up," Kelli replied. "If a parent is late and the kid stayed back to help, we have no way of knowing if he was with a teacher or if the parent picked him up. I'm really sorry."

"But don't you think it's odd that Layton came up with the tennis coach?" Jill said again, with a strange look on her face.

Kelli gave an internal sigh of exasperation. This woman was repeating herself as if trying to get Kelli to go along with some story.

"She was essentially insinuating that an innocent man had done something to her child," Kelli says, "and I wasn't going to go along with it."

"I'm really sorry," Kelli said again to Jill Easter. She felt that she might be apologizing too profusely, but she wanted to make sure the mom knew that Kelli took her distress seriously.

"I'm not blaming you at all," Jill said. "I just don't understand why he was brought up by the tennis coach."

"The coach brought Layton up because he's your son's teacher," Kelli said patiently. "Since Layton just took an hourlong tennis lesson with the coach, maybe he stayed back to help him. Have you asked your son?"

"I don't need to. He should have already been up front. The coach shouldn't have brought him around!"

"The coach did what we all do," Kelli replied. "When we see kids lag behind, we bring them up so they can reunite with their parents."

"All right," Jill said. She leaned in and lowered her voice. "I'm not accusing you of anything or blaming you."

"Okay," Kelli said, wondering what she could be possibly blamed for, as she'd done nothing wrong. "I just want to make sure you're okay. Are you good?"

"Yes, I'm good," Jill said.

Kelli looked over at Layton, who looked uncomfortable and embarrassed. Kelli felt sorry for him at that moment, because he was only six years old and didn't know what was going on. She didn't try to hug him like she normally would have because the moment didn't seem right, especially with Jill hovering in such an overprotective manner. Layton wasn't cowering or afraid of Kelli or anyone else, as Jill claimed. Instead, his countenance was resigned and a little embarrassed.

"Thanks," Jill said, and left with her son.

Kelli wondered if she should have addressed the fact that Jill was late and had actually created the situation. Instead, she shrugged it off. She wasn't one to rub parents' noses in their bad behavior. She again returned to the cooking class, shaking her head in confusion.

*Jeez, most parents apologize when they're late and hold their children accountable for not following the rules, instead of going around accusing volunteers like this Jill Easter woman.*

A few minutes later, she was once again called out by Janice, who looked frustrated.

"That mom wants to see you again."

"Oh, wow," Kelli said, surprised. She had the sinking feeling that all was not right with this mother. Jill seemed like a pit bull that had latched on to a bone and wouldn't let go.

In the hallway, Jill's face was dark and twisted. Her three kids were not with her. Kelli assumed they were now in the car alone while their mother paced in the hallway.

"Can I speak to you outside this time?" Jill asked.

"Sure," Kelli said, and followed her out the front door.

Jill sidled up to Kelli and lowered her voice conspiratorially. "Don't you think it's *odd* that my son was brought up *alone* by the tennis coach?"

"No, I don't think it's odd," Kelli said, biting her tongue against her impatience. *Why does she keep bringing this up?* She once again reiterated the facts: "If a child doesn't make it in the back door before it's locked, then they have to go around front. We're a family here, a team. Your son took a tennis lesson. That was his coach. His coach walked him to the front. Simple as that." She felt as though she was repeating herself over and over to this woman, but figured it might take a few tries to get through to her. Kelli continued doggedly. "If a child stays behind, then one of us will bring him up separately. It happens all the time. Yes, the policy is probably a little loose, but it works. We have never had a problem before. All the teachers and coaches look out for the kids here. We're a family, and having one of us bring up a straggler is a backup plan in case a kid stays behind."

"Well, then why was my son crying?" Jill said, her voice rising. "Something happened."

"I didn't see him crying," Kelli said, "but if he was before I saw him, it might have been because he thought he was going to get in trouble with you for not lining up. You're clearly angry. He wouldn't have gotten in trouble with me, though. That's not my role. I'm just the volunteer. If any of the kids get out of line, the coach or teacher will call the parents, or sometimes the principal steps in. But I never discipline the kids. So if Layton was crying because he thought he was going to get in trouble, it wouldn't have been because of me."

Jill glared at her. "It's really odd about the coach," she repeated in a strange, creepy voice. "Really, really odd. I don't like it."

Kelli met her eyes, unable to believe that this was actually happening. What kind of misunderstanding was this? This Easter woman seemed unable to see the situation for what it really was: a late parent and a kid slow to line up. Nothing had happened to Layton. The coach didn't do anything, and neither did Kelli. End of story.

Even if Layton had been crying as Jill claimed, there would have been no discipline from Kelli, no repercussions in any way for Layton.

"It wasn't my job to discipline the kids," Kelli says. "If there was ever an issue, that was for the teachers, administrators, or parents to handle. Volunteers just got to have fun."

Kelli's duties were limited to organizing, helping, cleaning, assisting the instructors, playing with the kids, taking roll, and bringing the kids to their waiting parents at the end of the day.

"Layton wasn't the only kid who took his time lining up, by the way," Kelli says. "Even my own daughter would take her time sometimes. That's what kids do. On those occasions when Syd would be slow to line up, I would tell her to hurry up, and then she would run in. She knew it was her responsibility first, and my responsibility second as her mom. It wasn't the volunteers' or coaches' responsibility to make sure all the kids lined up and were ready for pickup, although we did it to help out the parents and get the kids matched up."

Jill continued to glare at Kelli with narrowed eyes. "I think it's really strange that the coach was alone with my son." Her tone was low and accusatory. It gave Kelli chills. "I think the tennis coach molested my son."

Kelli gasped and stared at her.

*Is this woman really accusing an innocent man of child molestation?*

"Why would you say that?" Kelli said, her heart racing.

"Because his face is dirty," Jill said. "It looks like his face was forced down in the mud."

"No way," Kelli says. "I disagree. That did not happen and you know it. Why are you doing this? If Layton's face was dirty, it's because the kids play tennis on the black asphalt, and the tennis balls are covered in dust. It's hot, the kids are sweaty, they're wiping their faces, and they get dirty. There's no mud out there. There's no mud anywhere."

*What the hell? If this woman really thinks her son was molested, why is she standing here talking to me? Why isn't she calling the police or taking Layton to the hospital?*

"The only reason she was interrogating me like that," Kelli says, "was to try to get me corroborate the weird, crazy story she was concocting. Any mother who thinks their child has been molested gets help or goes to the authorities. She doesn't leave her supposedly traumatized, molested child alone in a car to go interrogate a school volunteer."

Jill crossed her arms and stared Kelli down. "He was molested," she insisted.

## "I'll Get You!"

*Oh my God.* A chill went down Kelli's spine. She knew the tennis coach well. He was a family man with children of his own whom Kelli had known for many years. He was a dedicated teacher who supported his family by coaching tennis at different places around Orange County.

"He was one of the nicest, most hardworking guys I knew," Kelli says. "This would have been a horrifying blow to him. He would have lost his livelihood and been unable to support his family. I wasn't going to let Jill Easter do this. I was ready to defend his character to the hilt."

Jill repeated her mantra six or seven more times. Kelli continued to deny any possibility of what Jill was saying.

Kelli says, "She was accusing the coach of the lowest thing a man who works with children could get accused of. She did it without giving a moment's thought to what she could do to this man's life."

When Kelli refused to give in, Jill stared at her with cold blue eyes and a calculating expression on her face. Kelli got the vivid sense that this was a woman who was used to bullying people to get what she wanted. She was clearly used to getting her way.

When Jill started up again, Kelli finally grew tired of her rant. She interrupted and said, "You know, I'm not doing this. I don't get paid for this. I'm just a volunteer. I don't know what you're trying to do. The coach is the most amazing man; he's got five minutes to pack up and leave. I'm not doing this. This is crazy. I'm not doing it. Goodbye." Then she turned around and walked away.

Behind her, Jill shouted in an enraged voice, "How do you sleep at night?"

Kelli ignored her and opened the door to return back inside.

Jill screamed behind her in a shrill, piercing tone, *"I'll get you!"*

Kelli froze in her steps. Her shoulders went up, a chill raced down her spine, and the hairs at the back of her neck stood up.

She'd never heard a tone like that before, or such frightening words: *"I'll get you!"*

Those words were a direct threat.

A very real, frightening threat from the mouth of an unstable woman.

# eight

"I'll get you!" Those words shook Kelli Peters to the core. All her life, she'd never had that kind of fear come over her. Nor had she ever had a confrontation like what she'd just experienced with Jill Easter.

Kelli prided herself on getting along with people. She was, as she describes in her own words, "a super chill, mellow person." She'd had minor disagreements in the past, yes, but she was always able to get beyond them with people.

She'd never had anything go this far, to this level.

Yet here she was, having a woman scream at her, "I'll get you!" all because she wouldn't go along with Jill's insinuations.

After Jill shrieked at the top of her lungs, "I'll get you!" a woman named Claire approached Kelli.

"Wow!" she said. "What the heck was that? I heard that woman yelling at you. If you need my help as a witness, let me know."

"Thank you," Kelli said, feeling a flood of relief that someone else had witnessed the altercation and saw how over the top it was.

Unfortunately, Claire moved out of the country shortly after the confrontation.

Kelli says, "She's been unreachable since. She didn't want to get involved once she saw the level to which Jill took the altercation. I also didn't want to call her and get her tangled up in something that seemed so petty."

Later, though, Kelli wished she had.

Little did she know that Jill Easter was about to wage a full-out war on her.

After the initial confrontation, Kelli burst into the office, her heart racing. The administrators rushed over to her.

"Are you okay?" they asked. "What just happened? We saw that woman yelling at you through the windows. What did she say to you?"

"She said she's going to get me," Kelli said, fighting back tears and trying not to hyperventilate. "She said, 'How do you sleep at night?' and 'I'll get you.'" Kelli's entire body trembled.

The administrators tried to comfort her and calm her down. "Kelli, you can't let this get to you. This kind of stuff happens from time to time with parents."

"Not like this," Kelli said. "She threatened me!"

"Don't worry about it; it'll blow over," the administrators said.

No one seemed to take Jill's words very seriously. Although it wasn't normal behavior for a parent to threaten a school volunteer over something so minor, anyone who had ever worked at a school knew that parents sometimes got emotional about issues related to their kids. The school administrators had seen their variety of problems, so the incident, while upsetting, didn't seem like anything that wouldn't blow over eventually. After all, what were the damages to Jill or her son? It all seemed like a minor misunderstanding.

Kelli called her ACE supervisor to tell her what had happened. The supervisor asked her to fill out an incident report.

"I was upset," Kelli says. "All I wanted to do was go home. But I had to fill out a detailed report documenting the incident. It was frustrating because in my mind, there was no incident, just Jill screaming at me."

After Kelli filled out the paperwork, she went about the rest of her day.

"At the time, I didn't outwardly take her words seriously," Kelli says, "but in my gut, I was uneasy. Something just didn't feel right with her."

The following afternoon, Kelli stood in front of the school office talking to the principal about what had happened the day before.

Two parents approached them. One of them was Kelli's friend Rita.

"Kelli," Rita said, "there's a blonde woman standing out front passing flyers out to all parents arriving for pickup."

Kelli's heart dropped to the floor.

*Jill Easter.*

*"I'll get you!"*

*She's making good on her threat.*

Kelli began to shake. "What? Are you sure?"

"Yes," Rita said with a look of chagrin on her face. She handed a flyer to Kelli, and another one to the principal. The principal immediately took the flyer from Kelli before she had a chance to read it. (Later, Kelli would hear that Jill, in the flyer, was asking for the school to remove Kelli as a volunteer for "intentionally" failing to follow ACE policies and "punishing" Layton. In the flyer, she accused Kelli of deliberately locking Layton out of the school and calling him "slow" to his face. She also accused Kelli of dragging Layton out back and bloodying his knuckles.)

"All lies," Kelli says. "I did nothing to that little boy. He was the sweetest little kid, and I loved him. No one ever hurt that child. If Layton was dirty, it was because he was playing tennis and collecting the balls off the ground, and then maybe he rubbed his face. He most definitely was not thrown facedown in the mud like Jill states, by myself or anyone else. I love children, and the thought of someone accusing me of hurting a child devastates me. I've cried myself to sleep countless nights at the thought of people possibly believing that of me. It's the furthest possible thing from who I actually am."

In front of the office, another mom walked up with a flyer in her hand. The principal grabbed it before Kelli could see it.

"Let me handle this," the principal said. "I'll take care of it."

"I was glad she grabbed the flyer," Kelli says. "I didn't want to see what was on it. My heart was beating so fast, and I felt shaky and sick to my stomach. I couldn't believe this woman was doing this. She was making good on her word that she would get me, all over a minor disagreement."

Kelli tried to go on with her day. She set up supplies for the art class and helped children in their other ACE classes, but all she could think about was what Jill Easter had done. The woman had actually made the effort to create and print flyers about Kelli, and then spent time passing them out to parents! Why take it to this level? Maybe it was because Kelli had told Jill she wasn't going to deal with her anymore, and that the whole thing was "crazy." She'd walked away from Jill, but was that enough to start passing out flyers to try and get her removed as a volunteer? Was that enough to damage her reputation in the community? It seemed so extreme. It didn't make sense.

Civil attorney Robert Marcereau later speculated, "Because Kelli hates confrontation and couldn't handle Jill yelling at her any longer, she walked away. Jill probably took that as being dismissed, and it angered her. Also, Kelli mentioned the word 'crazy,' which was a trigger for her."

There might have been an additional factor in Jill's behavior, however:

"At the time, we had no idea why she was constantly tardy," Kelli says. "When she arrived late that day, she looked guilty. Now I realize why she looked so sweaty and disheveled. She had the 'fresh-laid' look. It later came out in the police investigation and in court that Jill had been rushing to the school after an extramarital liaison with a firefighter. In hindsight, she might have been trying to create a diversion from her delay in picking up her child. She was having marital problems, an affair, and running late. She probably thought, *I'll put this off on other people, take the heat off me, and create a diversion so people don't ask where I've been.* In the drop of a word, she didn't think twice about ruining some poor guy's life by accusing him of child molestation. Nor did she think about what it would do to her son. Instead, it was about creating an issue to take the spotlight off why she was late. And then she changed her story, and I became her new target."

Kelli's friend Monique speculates: "I personally think Jill knew who Kelli was long before the confrontation. Kelli was bubbly, happy, and everyone liked her. The kids adored her. Even Layton, Jill's son, was always running to show her his art. He probably came home talking about Kelli. Kelli was the most popular volunteer in that school. I think Jill was watching from the sidelines in jealousy. I think she had it out for Kelli from the beginning."

That afternoon, Kelli went about her duties in the ACE program, but her stomach churned. Jill was still in front of the school, passing out flyers.

"I knew the principal was out there asking her to stop," Kelli says, "and that helped. I was glad for her support. I didn't want to see that flyer. It was too upsetting. From the bits and pieces I heard, it was disturbing and all lies. This chick clearly had it out for me, and it scared me to the bone. I couldn't believe that she had the balls to stand out front of a school spilling lies all over the place. In my mind, it seemed illegal. How could a woman blatantly spread lies about a person she didn't even know? Isn't that slander? I was absolutely terrified. I've never dealt with this level of crazy before, where someone was literally personally attacking me for no reason."

Later that day, the principal approached Kelli and told her that although she'd tried to make Jill stop passing out the flyers on school grounds, Jill had refused.

"She's not going to stop," the principal said. "She said she was utilizing her First Amendment right to freedom of speech."

"What should I do about this situation?" Kelli asked. "She's spreading lies. I feel like I should defend myself."

The principal then gave Kelli the best piece of advice that she would take with her from that moment on.

"Take the high road, Kelli," the principal said. "Walk away. Don't confront her. You're a representative of the school. Give her enough rope, and she'll eventually hang herself."

Kelli hung on to those words. "I wanted to go say something to Jill but never did, because first of all, it wasn't in my nature. I hate confrontation. Second of all, the principal's words stayed with me. Of course, don't get me wrong, there were times when Jill was out there spreading so many lies about me that I wanted to defend myself. There were other times I wanted to badmouth Jill back. I'm not a perfect person, and she was making me so angry with what she was doing. But instead, I took the principal's advice and let it run its course. Little did I know that it would take years, but I don't regret any of it. It was really Jill's battle alone. I didn't want to engage with her, and I had nothing against her, except for what she was doing to me. Can you imagine if I'd made my own flyers combating Jill's lies? It would've looked like there was a feud between the two of us, some sort of catfight, when that wasn't the case. Plus, it would have given her something on record to use against me in the future. I'm glad that I took the high road and never said anything, even though it was so difficult to hear someone slander me with outright lies and ruin my reputation. In the end, though, the principal was right. Jill did eventually hang herself with her own rope."

That evening, Kelli went home drained and exhausted. She told her husband about how this woman, Jill Easter, had passed out flyers full of lies about her.

Bill agreed that there was something very off about the entire situation.

"You need to be careful," he said. "She doesn't sound right in the head."

Kelli didn't sleep all night, tossing and turning as bad dreams wisped through her conscious.

"I was scared for my family," Kelli says. "My gut was telling me that something was really wrong with this cuckoo bird, and that I needed to be careful."

The following day, it was brought to Kelli's attention that Jill had called a bunch of school officials about the matter. The tennis coach was interviewed and said he'd been cleaning up and getting ready for his next job when he saw Layton Easter lagging behind. The child walked up to the back door to find it locked. The coach approached and told Layton he would bring him around front, which was normal procedure for ACE at that time. It had all happened exactly as Kelli had thought.

The police also investigated the incident and found no evidence of any wrongdoing on the parts of either the coach or Kelli.

After the flyer incident, word got out among parents and school employees. Everyone was talking about Jill Easter and her actions, and wondering aloud what had really happened between the two women. Over the next few days, Jill stopped passing out flyers. Instead, she took to standing out front of the school during pickup and telling everybody who passed that Kelli had hurt her child.

"She may as well have had a bullhorn," Kelli says, "she was so determined to get her point across. She kept repeating her latest story, which, of course, had changed once again. Now she was saying that I'd purposely dragged her child out of the school to punish him and bloodied his knuckles."

When Jill approached one of Kelli's friends with this accusation, Annette said, "Are you serious? The Kelli I know would never do something like that."

There were other parents at the school who didn't know what to believe, though. Jill was relentless with her campaign. People started looking at Kelli askance or avoiding her altogether. Every day, when she would walk down the hallways, she would see groups of women standing together, whispering and looking her way.

"It was hard," Kelli says. "Anybody Jill could talk to, she would. Some people didn't want to get involved or get on the bandwagon, and many others thought she was cuckoo right off the bat. Still, there were people who were interested in what she was saying and enjoyed the gossip and drama of it all. They became Jill's cronies and stirred the pot along with her. That hurt."

Jill also called Kelli's supervisor at the afterschool program, Irvine Public School Foundation, to try to get her removed. Jill told the IPSF supervisor, Stephanie, that her son wouldn't be returning to the program if Kelli remained as a volunteer.

Stephanie said, "Kelli is the best volunteer we have. I won't remove her until we do a full and complete investigation. I would be happy to refund your money in the meantime."

That wasn't good enough for Jill Easter. She was frustrated with her lack of progress. She sent multiple letters to the principal, demanding action. She wanted Kelli banned from everything—the PTA, art program, Plaza Vista, and the school district—all on the grounds that Kelli had supposedly "manhandled" her son.

When the principal refused to bow to Jill's demands and remove Kelli from her volunteer position, Jill went up the ladder of the school district. She filed complaint after complaint to the higher-ups. She also got her husband, Kent Easter, involved, and he began filing his own complaints, too, even though he'd never met Kelli.

Both the principal and the IPSF supervisor were fielding calls daily from the school officials. The situation was investigated repeatedly, with everyone involved interviewed multiple times. Every complaint was investigated by the school district and dismissed.

"They found there was no mishap," Kelli says. "They weren't going to remove me."

As word circulated about the drama between Jill and Kelli, one of the casualties was the reputation of the ACE program.

"During that time," Kelli says, "I noticed a decline in enrollment for our afterschool program. It went down by about twenty percent. It broke my heart. Jill had successfully smeared the program's reputation. She made people think that the volunteers or teachers weren't properly looking after kids. It wasn't true. There were the most dedicated people in that program, such hardworking, devoted people. We were all there because we believed in it, and because we loved children. The scandal created by Jill really affected that program. Most of all, it affected the kids."

Kelli was so devastated by the numbers that she offered to step down as the director of the art program.

"I felt I had to do something to save the program," she says. "My daughter and all the other kids loved that place. I didn't want to see it suffer because of something I was involved in, even though everything Jill was saying was all lies."

When Kelli tried to resign, both the ACE coordinator and head director of IPSF refused to accept her resignation.

"We need you," they said. "You're the lifeblood of this program at Plaza Vista."

So Kelli stayed on, but with mixed feelings. She hated the negative attention such a wonderful program was getting. She despaired that she had any part in that, even one as unfortunate as being at the wrong place at the wrong time to encounter Jill Easter.

In the meantime, Jill wasn't content with the harm she had already done. For the next six months, she continued to make up ever-changing lies about Kelli and the event. The situation escalated as Jill figured out new ways to stick it to Kelli.

"I would see her at the school on a daily basis," Kelli says, "and she would shoot me the nastiest looks. She would send her family members to pick up her kids, and they were constantly staring at me. It was upsetting to watch her gossip about me to anyone who would listen. Not only was she talking to everyone at school about me, she started going through the neighborhoods where we lived and spewing her nonsense, too. She talked to every single one of her neighbors about me. I would see some of these parents later at school, and they started giving me strange looks and avoiding me as if I were the plague. Jill was telling everyone who would listen that I hurt children and wasn't fit to be around kids. It was the most painful thing in the world."

Every time a new accusation would come out, the school officials would have to investigate all over again.

Kelli says, "They would tell me, 'We support you, but we have to ask you these questions.' And then we would go through it all over again: 'Are you sure you didn't call her son mentally slow, not just slow to line up?' 'She's claiming you deliberately locked her son out to punish him. Did you lock the door on him at any time?' It just never ended. I was having to tell my story over and over again."

One of the things that most upset Kelli was Jill's latest falsehood: that Layton had cowered when Kelli went to hug him.

"It was a blatant lie," Kelli says. "Jill makes up these anecdotes that paint a picture in someone's mind, and it's always the most awful picture. She was saying the worst things anyone can say about a mother or someone who works with children on a daily basis. That Kelli she was describing is someone I would never want to know or be around."

As the months passed, Kelli would hold her head up high and try to focus on her volunteer duties at the school. She would be working on a project, glance up, and see Jill Easter staring in the window at her. When Jill caught Kelli's eye, she would hold up her middle finger.

"She would flip me off constantly," Kelli says. "It was upsetting."

Whenever Kelli passed Jill in the hallway, Jill glared, her face twisted in disgust, and muttered vitriol. Kelli often saw Jill standing in groups of women, talking animatedly and pointing at Kelli. All of the women would turn to look at Kelli as she passed.

"The teachers told me she was talking to them, too," Kelli says. "It was so junior high. It made it hard to concentrate on my work."

Kelli began to worry that Jill's gang of friends would jump her if she were ever alone.

"I was frantically staying away from her," Kelli says, "and constantly watching my back. I enlisted my friends to help me with volunteering because I was afraid to be alone. I was worried that one of her friends would come up and hit me or start a fight. I'm only five feet tall and under a hundred pounds. Jill is a big woman, and all she had to do was get me alone and beat the crap out of me. I ended up carrying pepper spray because I knew it would be the only way I could ever get out of a situation if I had to."

Soon, it was nearing the end of the school year, and things still had not cooled down. The "feud" between the two women was the talk of the community. Everywhere Kelli went, someone would approach her, curious to know the backstory. They would also tell her things that Jill was saying.

"Jill is telling people you hurt children and should be dismissed. Did you do something to her kid?"

"Jill says you berated her son and hurt him and harassed him. Is that true?"

"Did you say something to piss her off? People don't just get that mad for no reason."

"What did you do to her son?"

"What did you do to *her*?"

Kelli answered the questions the best she could, but she could see the doubt lingering in people's eyes. It was difficult to see fellow parents trying to sort out truth from fiction.

She began to receive hateful emails in both her personal and PTA inboxes. The threats were written from fake accounts and said things like, *You'd better hope that I never run into you in a dark alley*, or, *You're lucky it wasn't my child you hurt because I would handle this myself*, or, *Why are you still here?*

It weighed heavily on Kelli's mind that Jill had people on her side that were sending hate mail without knowing the facts. "It dumbfounded me that people believed her lies."

Kelli contacted the police and gave them the emails. "I feared for my life and my family's life, so I was trying to give them evidence in case something happened."

The police investigated every single one of the emails.

"Those people may not know this now, but they were all investigated," Kelli says. "I know the name of one of the women who sent me the most hate mail. Her name was Dorothy. If I ever meet her one day, I'll say, 'Hi, Dorothy. You owe me an apology.'"

Jill continued demanding that Kelli be "fired." By that time, the people at the school were starting to roll their eyes.

"We all used to kind of laugh about it," Kelli says. "I'd been cleared multiple times. It was pretty obvious that Jill wasn't going to get me 'terminated' from my volunteer position, no matter how much she tried. The principal and Stephanie would say, 'Sheesh, you're not even an employee. We don't have any right over you. We can't fire someone who isn't even on payroll.'"

All this did was enrage Jill Easter.

"She began making up wilder and wilder lies," Kelli says, "like saying I abused children. That was the worst part. I would never hurt a child. I love children more than anything. For her to make those accusations that people could possibly believe was devastating to me."

The constant scrutiny began to wear on Kelli.

"I was crying all the time," she says. "Not just at home. I would break down at school, too. People would often ask me if I was okay. I was unable to sleep through the night anymore. I would get up every morning, hours before my family, and sit on the couch and cry uncontrollably. It was something I couldn't help. The stress and tension and lack of sleep would build up, and I had to release it. But I couldn't let my family see. It was so important to keep my anxiety from my daughter. She was already showing signs of stress herself. All the chatter at the school and the rumors were starting to trickle down to the kids, and some of them were being very mean to Sydnie. I needed her to have peace at home. I would get up extra early so that I could manage the stress before my family got up. It took an hour sometimes. Then I would get in the shower and clean up, and then wake everyone up for school and work. I would pretend like nothing was wrong and get Syd to school, get Bill off to work, and get on with my day."

Then Jill filed a restraining order against Kelli. In the document, she accused Kelli of threatening to kill her, threatening to approach and interrogate Layton, stalking her, and attempting to intimidate Layton. In the restraining order, Jill wrote, *I want her to discontinue telling parents at my school that I'm psychotic and unstable and spreading lies about me at school.*

Kelli couldn't believe the accusations in Jill's restraining order.

"That freaked me out," she says. "Everything that she said I was doing, was what she was doing."

The restraining order was thrown out by the court.

A month later, Jill filed her first round of lawsuits. She filed lawsuits against Plaza Vista Elementary School, the Irvine School District, IPSF, and Kelli personally. One of the lawsuits was even from her six-year-old son, Layton. Jill also sued "20 Jane Does" that were listed on the document. Neither Kelli nor the school administrators knew who the "20 Jane Does" were, but speculated they must be other random people at the school, possibly Kelli's friends or other school officials. It appeared Jill Easter was going to serve anybody she could.

"It scared everybody," Kelli says. "Everyone at the school started thinking they were going to get served with papers, just for knowing me. I felt really bad for my friends. It was as if they were guilty just for hanging out with me. Jill did this on purpose. It was psychological warfare."

The principal, for her part, stood strong in support of Kelli.

"We'll fight this together," she said. "You're not going anywhere, and I support you."

Kelli stayed on at the school, which enraged Jill.

It was at that time that Kelli found out that the Easters were attorneys who had gone to top schools. Kent went to Stanford undergrad and UCLA law school. Jill received both undergraduate and law degrees from UC Berkeley. They'd met at a law firm in Northern California. Kent was now a securities litigation partner at a top law firm in Orange County.

"They were powerful people," Kelli says. "I was worried that they would succeed. I didn't have money and knew nothing about the law, and they knew that."

The multiple, never-ending lawsuits had upped the ante. Kelli couldn't believe that Jill Easter had gone this far.

"I couldn't handle it," Kelli says. "When she filed that first lawsuit against me, I couldn't believe this was happening. It felt so awful, so surreal. I began to question myself. What did I do to cause Jill to be this angry? Was there something I said that set her off like this? I racked my brain over and over, going over every single detail of our encounter. There was nothing I could come away with that explained her level of rage against me. If I'd truly done something that caused her to get that pissed off, I would have apologized. I wanted this to go away. I wanted this to be resolved. I wanted to talk to her to try to work it out, but was advised by everyone not to. I wasn't dealing with a rational person, they said. It'll only make it worse. I didn't know what to do."

The principal, superintendent, and director of the afterschool program were all understandably upset about the lawsuits as well. Not only would the lawsuits take up valuable time and resources, but it looked bad for Plaza Vista Elementary School and the district.

"Those multiple, ongoing lawsuits told the real story about Jill Easter," Kelli says. "First, she'd made up a story about the coach that I wouldn't support, then she went after an underfunded public school supported by tax dollars, then she went after an afterschool program that's funded by parents for children, and then she went after me, a volunteer who spends her time for free at the school and lives month to month financially. But Jill had no problem suing everyone and trying to take their money. She had no problem taking money away from children. She wasn't getting her way, so she was going to use her power and money as an attorney, and her husband's power and money, to bully everyone. She was willing to go that far to have me removed, just for sport. Maybe it's because she felt she had nothing to risk. She didn't care about anyone she hurt, most of all the children who were going to lose out by her actions."

After Jill began filing lawsuits, Kelli had to repeatedly sit down with school attorneys and go over every detail of her conversation with Jill that had sparked it all. The meetings lasted hours and took time away from volunteering and family life. The attorneys questioned her over every aspect of the confrontation. No stone was left unturned.

Kelli says, "They would ask repeatedly, 'Why is this woman in such an uproar over you? What did you do to her? How many encounters have you had with her? Is this an ongoing feud?' I would answer every single question, telling them repeatedly that I'd only met her once, that we'd only had a short conversation, and that there was no ongoing feud. The officials interviewed the principal and witnesses and everyone else involved, and they kept coming up with the same conclusion. They would say, 'There's no obvious violation here,' and tell Jill that her claims and repeated lawsuits had no basis."

Luckily for Kelli, the school district allowed her to retain legal representation free of charge.

"I never could have afforded to fight the Easters otherwise," Kelli says. "The school's attorneys defended both the district and me. It was very comforting. That was another reason I didn't just disappear. I felt safe at the school. The administrators were clearly on my side and became my family."

The Easters weren't deterred. The lawsuits kept coming.

"It almost seemed like a game to them," Kelli says. "They had no problem abusing the system and taking up the court's time. So far, nothing Jill or her husband had done to get me kicked out had worked. I knew they were pissed. They kept filing more lawsuits and using their power as attorneys to bully me."

During it all, Kelli found a measure of comfort in seeing the familiar faces at Plaza Vista every day. The brick building, the parents dropping off their kids, the hustle and bustle of a busy school day—all of it gave Kelli a feeling of normalcy. The children were the best part.

"Seeing their sweet, smiling faces kept me going," Kelli says. "It was another reason why I couldn't leave. Those children gave me strength."

By far the biggest reason Kelli stayed at the school, however, was because she was worried about her daughter's safety. If Jill Easter was this deluded, this destructive, this *determined*, to what lengths would she go to hurt Kelli? Would she harm Sydnie to hurt Kelli? Anything seemed possible.

"I was too afraid to go home," Kelli says, "and I didn't want to be away from Sydnie. So I started spending all my time at the school. That must've enraged Jill to see me there even more than before. But I felt as long as I was at school, I was with Sydnie and could keep an eye on her. I knew that if Jill and Kent Easter really wanted to hurt me, the quickest and most evil way would be to do something to my child. I watched Syd like a hawk and never let her out of my sight. She wasn't allowed to play outside anymore—this little girl who'd loved being outdoors so much. It changed Sydnie's life in the biggest way, and this was just the beginning. I felt in my heart that Jill was waiting to kidnap my little girl if I let my guard down. That's how angry this woman was at me for something I didn't even do. I knew at this point that she and Kent would stop at nothing. They'd gone so far already, and I was still at the school, and that made them furious."

Kelli noticed that Sydnie was starting to lose some of her happy-go-lucky nature. She was becoming quiet and withdrawn. Word about the "conflict" was on everyone's lips, including the children's, and Syd's classmates began to treat her differently.

Things changed at home, too. Before, Kelli and Syd had loved to cook fresh, homemade dinners every night together. That fell by the wayside as Kelli coped with the stress of Jill Easter's harassment. Everything was taking a back seat to emotional survival. Some days, all Kelli had the energy for was ordering delivery or opening a can of soup for her family.

"Jill's harassment started to change the way I took care of my family," Kelli says. "I was barely getting through the day. There wasn't much left over because I was dealing with such emotional turmoil."

Then Kelli began to suspect that Jill was stalking her.

"I had this horrible feeling that she was watching me and following me," Kelli says. "The police later told me it was true."

Sometimes Kelli saw what appeared to be Jill's car following her. Other times, she glimpsed Jill's face in crowds. One time, at Costco, she heard Jill's shrill laugh behind her. Sure enough, Jill Easter just happened to be there at the same time and place as Kelli.

Kelli changed the locks on her doors and stopped driving at night. On the rare occasions when she did have to drive, she would panic the whole time. Instead of walking her dogs in beautiful Irvine, Kelli was afraid to take them out alone. The quiet streets, once so peaceful, now felt ominous. Kelli called and texted friends every day to ask them to come with her when she walked the dogs.

"My friends would take turns helping me," Kelli says. "I was constantly looking over my shoulder. I cried when I walked the dogs. I felt like I was putting my friends in danger. They were actually worried at times for themselves, but they never left me. They would walk me all the way to my door. I'm so grateful to my friends Rachel and Cherie for making sure I felt safe. I know that they were frightened, too, by this whole experience. It was out of everyone's comfort zone. None of us had ever experienced something like this before. But even despite the weirdness of it all, my friends never left my side."

Through it all, Kelli kept showing up at the school, day after day.

"I had obligations," Kelli said, "and I wasn't going to let Jill and Kent take that away from me."

Still, despite her outward stoicism at school—which some say drove Jill into a frenzy of rage—Kelli was barely surviving each day.

"I was having anxiety attacks," Kelli says. "They would come on at any given time. I would be walking down the hall with a teacher and just start shaking or crying. I had no control of my emotions anymore."

All day long, Kelli's friends would check up on her. At any given time, she had about fifteen friends in rotation. They would look out for her and stay actively by her side to make sure she made it through the day.

She began to experience severe physical symptoms. "I would shake uncontrollably. I started to talk to myself. I would completely tune out my surroundings and start having a dialogue with myself, telling myself to be strong and that I would get through it. I would pretend that people were asking me about the situation, and I had to defend myself. During those times, I didn't notice if anyone was around. This—talking to myself—had never happened before, and it terrified me. I felt like I was losing my mind."

Often, Kelli would be explaining things to an invisible accuser and then end up burning dinner.

"Sydnie would stare at me," Kelli remembers. "She had this look of such worry on her face. She would be talking to me, and I would be in a fog and not even hear her. I barely remember seeing her at that time. This was the daughter I'd been so involved with, so connected to on every level, and now she was almost invisible to me as I tried to cope with this onslaught."

Over the next six months of constant harassment, Kelli's quality of life went down. She rarely slept and was barely able to consume food.

"I started losing weight," she says. "My hair began to thin and fall out in clumps. My scalp showed through. I felt so ugly. I stopped doing my hair or getting dressed the way I used to. I just became so depressed."

The few hours of sleep she did get every night were filled with terrible dreams.

"I had constant nightmares about Jill," Kelli says. "They were always the same. I dreamt she was going to sneak into my bedroom and slit my throat. I began sleeping with a blanket up to my neck. The thought of Jill cutting my throat became my worst fear. Those nightmares were constant and felt so real. I became terrified to have my neck exposed, even during waking hours."

Kelli began knitting herself scarves to cover her neck. She was on a budget, so she made them herself instead of buying them. She didn't wear the scarves out in public, though, especially since the weather had warmed up. She didn't want to seem paranoid. Instead, she wore the scarves around the house, at every moment except showering.

"It made my neck feel less exposed," Kelli says. "I know it sounds crazy, but those nightmares felt so real."

Still, the fear lingered. Whenever Kelli was in public and talking to someone, she would instinctively hold her neck. "I was terrified that someone would come up behind me and cut my neck. I would get the worst heebie-jeebies, and no one knew. The only outward sign I gave was holding my neck."

In June, the PTA planned an end-of-the-year party and barbecue at a community pool across the street from the school. All of the children from Plaza Vista were invited.

Even though Kelli knew Jill Easter might be there, she reluctantly decided to attend for her daughter. Kelli's stomach was in knots as she walked into the party. She was relieved to see a group of people she knew, all sitting together: school acquaintances, friends, school administrators, and the principal. She joined the group, who immediately brought her into the fold. It was comforting to be with a group of friends who supported her.

At first, Kelli didn't see Jill Easter at the party. She started to relax, hoping that maybe her nemesis wouldn't show up. She talked with the other moms about their kids and their plans for the summer. Even though she was socializing as if everything was okay, she felt removed, as if she were observing herself with a third eye. She'd been through a war zone—was still immersed in it—and felt emotionally drained. It was hard to be cheery and happy with so much on her mind.

Then she saw her.

Jill Easter.

Jill was playing in the pool with her kids. Kelli quickly scanned the area. She didn't see any of Jill's friends.

Kelli was surprised that she'd had the guts to show up alone. "Considering the campaign of harassment that Jill had engaged in against me and the school for the past months, it took some serious balls to go to that party alone. The entire administration was there. I had to give her credit."

Kelli's stomach knots came back, and she began to shake. The women in her group noticed and began talking her through it.

"You're with us," they said. "She can't do anything."

"I think I should leave," Kelli said. "I don't want to be anywhere near her."

"Don't let her run you off. Stay for a little while longer. We have your back."

"Okay," Kelli said reluctantly. Out of the corner of her eye, she could see Jill frolicking with her kids in the water. She seemed to be playing to an audience, which was typical of her. She was horsing around in the water in an exaggerated way, as if aware that eyes were on her. She wrestled with her kids and splashed them, a huge smile plastered on her face. She laughed a little too long and loudly at their antics. It was as if she were putting on a show, saying, "Look at me! Look at what a good mom I am and how much fun I'm having! Look at how carefree and unaffected I am by everything I've done!"

"Her children seemed a bit bewildered by her efforts," Kelli says, "but also happy to join in."

Everyone in Kelli's group was now watching Jill. The administrators were careful not to say anything, but everyone was thinking the same thing: *Here's the woman who has made our lives living hell for the past months, taunting us with her presence and behavior.*

A different group of women sitting nearby—parents Kelli didn't know—began to say things under their breaths, snarky comments about Jill and her arrogance. Some of them snickered. Kelli and her friends immediately felt uncomfortable. They didn't want to partake in the same behavior that Jill was guilty of. This wasn't a catfight between them where everyone drew lines in the sand and took sides. While Kelli appreciated the support from these women she didn't know, she didn't want things to go this way. This wasn't a game. It wasn't a joke. She didn't want to infuriate Jill further and cause potential danger to Kelli and her family. She was glad her own friends, representatives of the school, were keeping it respectful and not saying anything. However, Kelli could see that Jill was seething because it appeared Kelli had a huge group of friends and supporters, and Jill didn't. Kelli's stomach turned over.

"I need to go," she said, gathering her things. The situation didn't feel right. She scanned the pool for Sydnie. All Kelli could think about was getting away from Jill as quickly as she could.

"Don't go," her attorney friend said. "She can't do anything."

"I really need to leave," Kelli said.

"But you just got here. Sydnie's having fun."

Kelli spotted Syd laughing and playing with her friends, and her heart clenched. It had been so long since she'd seen Syd smile. Her daughter had been through so much emotional turmoil in the past few months. It seemed unfair to drag her away.

"Okay, I'll stay a little bit longer," Kelli said. Out of the corner of her eye, she saw that Jill was now in the Jacuzzi. She was talking to people and glaring over at Kelli with a nasty expression.

Kelli's heart sank. *Here we go again.*

"I'm heading over there to hear what she's saying," one of the women in Kelli's group said.

"I'll go with you," said another.

The two women got up and went over to the hot tub, where they sidled up next to Jill. They later said they'd walked up on Jill engaged in negative talk about Kelli.

Of course.

That was what Jill did.

But the snarky comments in Kelli's group had turned this into something Kelli never wanted: furthering Jill's perception that Kelli was her enemy.

At that moment, Kelli's gut told her that if Jill had declared war before, it was now going to be an all-out nuclear attack.

"If Jill had been a normal person," Kelli says, "I would have gone over there and invited her to join our group, invited her to have a hot dog with me. I would have said, 'Let's put this behind us, let bygones be bygones,' even though it was never my war to begin with. Even after everything that she'd done, I could have found some sort of forgiveness. But unfortunately, Jill had proven with her extreme behavior that she wasn't a reasonable or rational person. Even though every bone in my body wanted to reach out to her and try to mend this, I knew it wouldn't do an ounce of good. She's the kind of person who perceives kindness as weakness. I was also being advised by the school attorneys and my lawyer friends to not talk to Jill and to avoid her completely. So I did."

Kelli stayed at the party for a while longer, then finally collected Sydnie to go. As she was leaving, she saw Jill watching her with narrowed eyes.

Kelli could only imagine what was to come.

Much to Kelli's surprise, however, the harassment stopped. When school started up again in July (Plaza Vista was a year-round school), Kelli noticed that Jill was avoiding her. In fact, she didn't see much of Jill Easter at all after that.

The gossip stopped. The police reports stopped. The lawsuits stopped. The glares and obscene gestures and bullying all stopped, as did the anonymous emails.

Everything went quiet for six months. Not a peep was heard from Jill or Kent Easter.

Kelli took a deep breath, wondering if Jill was finally satisfied with the pound of flesh that she and her husband had extracted. Could the Easters have finally gone away? It seemed too good to be true, but Kelli was grateful for the reprieve.

"I started to gain my confidence back," she says. "I started driving at night again and walking my dogs without my friends by my side. I tried to ignore my gut feeling that I shouldn't let me guard down. I wanted my normal life back so badly, though. Before I met Jill, I used to go to the dog park every day after school with Sydnie and our dogs, but I'd cut down on that because I was too frightened to drive there. I'd stopped doing all the things I loved. But now, I wanted to get back into my old routine, and part of that was taking the dogs to their park after Syd got out of school. This whole thing had become so unfair to my dogs, too. I wanted to make it up to them and start giving them more outdoor time again."

One day a teacher friend of Kelli's needed someone to look after her youngest son after school, so she reached out to Kelli. Kelli immediately jumped at the chance.

"I would pick up the teacher's son after ACE, collect Sydnie and the dogs, and head over to the dog park," Kelli says. "It was such a quiet thrill to be asked to care for a friend's child. It meant the world to me. It meant there were people who didn't believe the bullshit Jill had spread about me. My reputation was everything to me, and had been basically ruined because of Jill Easter. So when a friend enlisted my help, it meant so much. I needed to be trusted. I hadn't done anything wrong, but it didn't matter. I was feeling awful about myself, and it showed. The day my teacher friend asked me to take care of her son was completely uplifting. I started to feel better about myself. I thought, *Maybe my life can start to get back to normal.*"

The dog park was a community of its own, with a close-knit group of people who'd known Kelli for more than ten years. Every night, the dogs would frolic together on the grass, the kids would play, and the adults would talk and share in each other's lives.

"We were such a family," Kelli says. "All of us knew each other well, and we looked forward to getting updates on things that were happening in each other's lives. Those people had my back, and I had theirs."

One day, six months after the initial confrontation with Jill Easter, something strange happened. While Kelli was talking to her friends while the dogs ran and scampered, a short older woman with frizzy brown hair approached Kelli. It was out of the blue. Kelli had never

## "I'll Get You!"

seen this woman before. The woman carried a purse, which struck Kelli as strange, since no one ever brought a purse to the dog park.

Even odder: the woman didn't have a dog.

"She tried to start a conversation with me," Kelli says, "and tried a little too hard to be friends with my dog, Stanley. The weird thing was, she did this with no one else's dog but mine. Plus, she was at a dog park with no dog!"

The woman showed her teeth in a big smile that seemed forced. As she spoke to Kelli, she gazed at her intently in a way that sent a chill down Kelli's spine. The woman then pulled something out of her pocket that she seemed to have too conveniently ready.

"Here's my card," the woman said, still grinning brightly. "I'm a dog sitter. Please let me know if you need me for anything. Anything at all. I would be glad to help with your dog. I would be glad to come to your house."

Kelli asked her some questions. "I asked her how much she charged, if she had references, things like that. She had a nice, quick answer for everything. She kept saying she would love to come to my apartment and watch my dog there. I thought that was so strange. Usually we would drop our dogs off at a friend's house or a business, not have a stranger pop up out of nowhere and offer to come into my home. I told her, 'Thanks for the card. I'll call you if I need you, but I already have someone.' That woman didn't offer her services to anyone else that day. She came by herself and sought me out with obvious intentions."

After the woman left the dog park, Kelli's friends gathered around her. They conversed about what they'd just seen, and how it was clear that the woman was trying to get into Kelli's home.

"That would not be the only time I would see her," Kelli says. "She followed me in her car often."

One day, Kelli was at an Irvine lake with Stanley and the woman darted across the grass toward her.

"Oh my goodness," the woman said effusively, "I can't believe I ran into you again. What a coincidence! Remember me? I met you at the dog park!" She leaned down to pet Stanley, gushing over him. "Hello there, Stanley, my buddy. So good to see you, Stanley!"

Kelli felt an immediate rush of terror. Her legs almost buckled beneath her.

"I thought I was going to die that day," she says. "There was something so creepy about her, and she'd been following me. I thought the Easters had hired her to do something to me. I was so terrified that I couldn't move. I couldn't talk. All I could do was stand there, frozen, while she blabbered on about what a coincidence this was and how much she loved Stanley."

Kelli finally found her bearings and told the woman she had to go. She rushed away as quickly as she could, afraid to look back for fear the woman was following her.

When Kelli got to her car, she jumped in and locked the doors. Then she called Detective Andreozzi and told him about the woman.

Later, Kelli would learn that the woman was a private investigator hired by the Easters. She was trying to get access to Kelli's home on behalf of the Easters, just as Kelli and her friends had suspected.

"At that point," Kelli says, "I became completely paranoid again. I'd been trying not to let my worry and fears get the best of me, but now there was no doubt that the Easters hadn't stopped after all. I'd wanted to continue living my life as normally as possible, but it wasn't going to happen."

The stalking didn't end there. Soon, Kelli began to notice a man in a white car following her every time she drove somewhere.

"I thought, *I can't believe this*," Kelli says. "I mean, my God, when is this going to end? No one is going to believe that I'm now being followed by some guy in a white car. I kept seeing him everywhere. I was living in a nightmare. I saw that man's car a lot, but each time forgot to get his license. I couldn't tell anyone. I figured people would think I'd completely lost my mind. I mean, I couldn't really prove at that time that the lady at the dog park was following me, even though I knew deep down that she was."

One day, the man in the white car followed Kelli as she walked her dog. He drove slowly next to her on the street, looking over at her. Kelli was about a mile from home when she saw him. A deep, skin-crawling panic came over her.

"I got so terrified that I ran," Kelli said. "I ran and ran, as fast as I could. I was freaking out. I ran to the apartment complex next to mine and called Bill. I screamed for him to come quickly, that someone was following me."

After she hung up, Kelli couldn't move. She began to sob loudly, her cries echoing off the nearby walls. She remained frozen in place until Bill finally arrived and rushed to get her.

"I told him about the guy in the white car," Kelli says. "I told him every detail about how he'd been following me. I wanted to call the police but felt as if no one would believe me. So I begged Bill to take me home. I'd begun to doubt myself. Was I having hallucinations? Was this real? I couldn't tell. I was really confused, and oh my God, I was so scared. I started looking at every white car after that. And let me tell you, there were so many white cars out there that I was always jumpy. It's no way to live."

Weeks went by, and the man in the white car started parking under Kelli's bedroom window. At first, she didn't know it was him. Then, one evening, she looked out her window and spotted him parked outside, peering up at her. Their eyes met for a long, spine-chilling moment, and then he started his car and drove away.

Kelli attempted to write down his license plate but couldn't see it through the dense trees.

A few weeks later, Kelli told the tennis coach about the man, and he said the same guy in the white car had been following him! The coach said he would approach their stalker the next time the coach saw him.

He soon had his opportunity. When the coach saw the man in the white car parked in front of his house, he walked up to the car and asked why he was following him.

"The man ended up getting out of the car and going into the coach's house," Kelli says. "They had a cup of coffee, and the man told the coach that the Easters had hired him to follow both him and me because they wanted to catch us having an affair. When the coach called me to tell me all this, I was floored! I'd been right! My gut had been telling me that I was being followed and in danger this whole time that the Easters were supposedly 'backing off,' and my instincts were right. I'd been going through all this weird paranoia but trying to get back to normal, but I'd always had this feeling that it wasn't over. Look at the level Jill had already taken this! I knew something wasn't right with this lady."

For Kelli, it was a terrifying feeling to know she'd been right all along.

"It had been a month of this weird gut paranoia," Kelli says, "thinking that people were following me, and yet feeling like I was going crazy. But I was wrong. The Easters weren't taking a break or backing off during that time. I was still on their radar."

It had been a year since Kelli's initial confrontation with Jill Easter.

Jill and Kent Easter had certainly not taken a break or backed off.

Nor had they gone away.

They were plotting their next move.

# nine

February 17, 2011, started out as an ordinary day for Kelli Peters. Life was beginning to get back to normal for her. There hadn't been any more harassment or incidents from Jill Easter for months. Kelli was spending quality time with her daughter again and getting back into her former pursuits. Best of all, she was starting to feel like her old self again, although a pervasive sense of unease still followed her at times.

On this particular Wednesday, she left her apartment at her usual time to volunteer, a little before 11:30 a.m. She liked to arrive early for the ACE program, well before the children arrived to their afterschool classes at one p.m.

She got into her vanilla PT Cruiser and drove the familiar way to Plaza Vista Elementary School, through the bucolic, eucalyptus-lined streets of Irvine. It was a beautiful day, crisp but sunny, with puffs of white clouds dotting the pale sapphire sky.

As Kelli drove, she looked in her review mirror and noticed a weather-beaten blue Honda four-door following close behind. With every turn that she made, the car did the same. She was barely able to make out the form of the person behind the wheel. He was a dark-haired man, hunching down behind the steering wheel in an obvious way, as if not to be seen.

A chill ran through Kelli. *Is he following me?*

As the old blue car continued to follow her PT Cruiser, a dismal feeling settled into her heart. *I thought it was over.* She'd hoped the Easters had finally gone away. But this blue car... Had they hired someone to follow her? Another PI? What next?

She pulled into the school parking lot with the blue car tailing close behind. The Honda then passed Kelli, made a sudden left turn in the parking lot, and drove the wrong direction in the designated lane, away from Kelli. Instead of following the clearly marked one-way lane for drop-off, the man in the Honda had chosen to drive the opposite way, much to the chagrin of the other arriving parents. There were always rule breakers or clueless parents during pickup and drop-off, but this seemed ridiculous. Going the wrong way in a clearly designated zone seemed to take some deliberate effort. Besides, the man didn't even have kids in his car.

Kelli considered the situation. Maybe it wasn't what she thought. Maybe this was a lost driver? Someone who wasn't even part of the school but wandered into the parking lot by mistake? It was possible.

The blue car continued on its way through the lot. Kelli got out of her car and greeted a friend. Together, they watched the car weave through the parking lot the wrong way with the man crouched low behind the wheel. He meandered through the lot, and then finally left the school.

As Kelli watched the blue car round the corner and disappear from sight, she breathed an internal sigh of relief. She looked at her friend and shrugged. "Probably someone lost."

"Yep," her friend said, but their eyes met for a long moment.

*What if...?*

Kelli shrugged her fears away. She didn't want to go there.

The past few months of peace had been so nice...she didn't want to reawaken the old paranoia and fear that had haunted her life for so long.

Still, as she walked through the halls on her way to the ACE program, a niggling worry tapped on the shoulder like an insistent toddler. Who was driving that Honda? And why had he followed her all the way from her apartment?

It seemed strange.

She clocked into the school computer, and then headed over to the ACE building to do some Meet the Masters art preparation before the children arrived. Since it was Wednesday, it was an early day for the kids.

Kelli set about preparing art supplies for the students, carefully arranging paintbrushes, watercolors, and papers on the desks. Keeping busy was always a good distraction whenever she felt anxiety creeping in. But despite her best efforts, the thought of that car gave her a knot in her stomach.

She took a deep breath and gave herself a pep talk. *It was probably nothing. Don't be paranoid. Focus on giving the students the best lesson possible. Don't give that car any more thought. Focus on the positive.*

She started to feel better. A sense of calm descended on her. She was tired of living her life looking over her shoulder. She wanted to get on with things.

Her phone rang. It was the karate instructor.

"Hey, Kelli," he said. "I'm stuck in some pretty bad traffic. Looks like there was an accident, and they've shut down the freeway. Can you cover for me until I get there?"

"Sure," Kelli said. "Don't worry, I have it under control." After she hung up, she left the art room to go round up the karate kids, who were now arriving in droves.

She led them into the multipurpose room and got them started on their warmup, which consisted of stretches and basic cardio.

While the karate kids were warming up, Kelli helped get all the children to their classes with the help of the other volunteers. Then she returned back to the multipurpose room.

The door opened, and one of the administrators entered.

"Kelli," she said, "the police are here to see you." She had an odd look on her face.

Kelli's stomach turned over. "The police?"

"Yes. They need to talk to you. I can take over the class and keep an eye on the children while you meet with them."

"Are you sure they want to talk to me?" Kelli stared at her in confusion.

"Yes," the administrator said in a serious tone. "They asked for you by name."

Kelli's heart thudded to the floor. *Something must've happened to Bill!* She flew through the doors and raced down the halls toward the office. Panic gripped her insides. *Please don't let it be Bill.*

As she ran through the school grounds, her heart beat wildly in her chest. *Is he injured? Or, God forbid...dead?* Why else would the police be there to see her?

*At least Syd is okay.*

Kelli clung to that thought. Her daughter was safe; she knew that much. Sydnie was back there in the ACE classroom, getting ready to draw in her cartooning class.

*Oh God, please let Bill be okay!*

All Kelli could do was hold on to hope as she raced through the halls.

Since she was at the far end of the school, it felt as though she were running in slow motion.

"I was all the way across campus in another building," she says. "I had to go through the back doors and down a long hallway to get to the front. It felt like the longest journey of my life. I knew in my heart something was terribly wrong."

When Kelli arrived at the front of the school, she saw an austere police officer waiting for her.

"Did something happen to my husband?" Kelli asked, fighting

back tears. Her stomach was twisted in knots.

"No," the officer said. He was a handsome, stern-faced man named Officer Shaver. "Nothing is wrong with your husband."

"Well...then what is it?"

"Someone called us and complained that you were driving erratically through the school."

Kelli almost laughed. That was absurd. "There's no way," she said. "I would never do that. There are speed bumps everywhere, and we discourage people from driving erratically. There are children here. I always look out for their safety. I would never do that."

"That's the call we got, ma'am."

"It just wasn't me. You have the wrong person."

"The caller told us it was you by name," the officer said.

Kelli gasped. "By name?"

"Yes, ma'am."

"What time did they say this happened?"

"1:15 p.m."

"Well, I arrived at the school at 11:30 and was in the office the whole time. At 1:15, I was getting the kids off to their classes. It just wasn't me."

Officer Shaver looked at her sternly. "I need you to get out your car keys, Mrs. Peters. I will accompany you to your vehicle so that you may open it for us to inspect, please."

"Okay," Kelli said. Confusion swirled through her brain. *What is happening?*

She fumbled in her purse for her keys, her hands shaking. When she found them, she gripped them as if they were a lifeline. The cold metal felt tangible and real—something to hold on to—in a situation that felt increasingly surreal.

*The cops are here to see me?* Kelli had always been law-abiding. This made no sense.

As they walked through the parking lot toward Kelli's PT Cruiser, a helicopter buzzed overhead.

*My God, a helicopter?*

She spotted a black-and-white police car with swirling lights parked in behind her PT Cruiser. It was blocking her in, as if she were some sort of dangerous criminal.

It all felt so dreamlike, so strange.

Kelli looked over at Officer Shaver. "Is there a dead body in my car or something?" She let out a nervous chuckle.

The officer turned and met her eyes. He did not smile. "Ma'am, somebody saw you place drugs in the back seat of your car."

Kelli's breath stopped in her chest.

*Drugs?*

She was the type of person who couldn't sleep if she got a parking ticket!

"That's untrue," Kelli told the policeman. Her voice trembled. "I don't do drugs. It's impossible that someone saw me do anything like that. When we get to my car, I'll prove it to you."

"Okay," Officer Shaver replied.

When they arrived at Kelli's PT Cruiser, she stopped dead in her tracks. Through the large back window of her vehicle, she saw a large bag of leafy-green marijuana on the back seat.

Her heart thumped wildly in her chest. *How can this be happening?*

The officer took her keys and opened her car door.

He held up the bag of marijuana. A few moments later, he pulled out a clear plastic baggie of white pills, followed by a marijuana pipe.

Kelli stared at the drugs in horror.

"Those aren't mine!" she said, sputtering. She sounded like every other criminal, of course, denying the clear evidence, the obvious proof. She saw how it must look to the cops. Still, she pressed on. She was innocent!

"They're not mine, I swear." She clasped her hands together to keep them from shaking. They were damp and clammy.

"Ma'am, we have some questions for you," Officer Shaver said, pulling out a pad and pen.

Kelli nodded, her brain suddenly numb. She felt as though she were operating in slo-mo.

*Am I in a bad dream? Is someone playing a prank on me?*

Kelli went over the possibilities in her mind. Maybe her friends were playing a joke on her. That had to be it. Maybe they were "punking" her, like that TV show that set people up? That was the only thing that made sense. Either that, or the police were somehow mistaken. They must've gotten the wrong person. There had to be a mix-up.

"At that point, I start to feel very out of control," Kelli says. "It felt like a bad dream. I wondered if I was having a nightmare. My mind started going over all the people that had been in my car recently. Had they done something weird? I immediately dismissed that thought, because the only people that had been in my car were little kids the night before. They were only six years old, so there was no explanation."

The police began asking questions. "Do you recognize these drugs? Do you know where they came from? Did you place them in your car?"

Kelli repeatedly told them no, they were not her drugs. The cops continue to interrogate her, asking the same questions over and over again.

"They were trying to see if I was lying," Kelli says. "They would ask me where I was on certain dates, and I just couldn't think. With every word, I felt as though I was sinking down further and further. It's a very hopeless feeling. When you're under so much stress, your mind plays tricks on you. I couldn't control my thoughts. At one point, I considered the possibility that I was a sleepwalker and had done something that I didn't remember. There really was no explanation I could think of for the drugs being in my car. I was desperately trying to think of something to tell them. I started talking out of control, saying, 'These aren't my drugs! I don't know how they ended up in my car. This has to be a mistake,' etc. I kept repeating myself like a broken record. At one point, they asked me to stop talking."

Amidst the questioning, Kelli glanced up to see her friend, Annette, drive by slowly in her car. Annette's brow was furrowed, her face pinched with confusion and worry. It suddenly struck Kelli how she must appear to passersby. She was surrounded by police officers, with a helicopter swirling overhead. She looked as though she'd done something wrong.

This was happening at one of the most important places in Kelli's life: her beloved school where she felt like somebody…where she had a purpose…where she felt at home.

"It was hard to control my tears at that point," Kelli says. "It started to dawn on me that people were watching. I saw people outside the school staring at me. I could see what they were thinking."

The police officers placed the drugs on the roof of the police car, in plain sight of all passersby. This was a busy time of day, with parents arriving to pick up their children.

"Those aren't my drugs," Kelli said again as tears flowed down her cheeks. "Please put them away."

"Ma'am, we have a job to do here," Officer Shaver said.

"Please put those drugs away! The kids will see them. My daughter is getting out of her class. Please!" Kelli was weeping now. She fell to her knees. Her loud sobs punctuated the quiet school grounds, echoing off the buildings. "You're going to ruin my life. I'm innocent, but this will still ruin my life. Please!"

"Ma'am, please calm down. We still have more questions for you."

Kelli began to scream. "I can't have my daughter seeing those drugs!" She was wailing now, so hysterical that it was hard to get the words out.

"We're going to have to ask you to be quiet, ma'am," Officer Shaver said in a firm voice. "Please get off your knees and take a seat on the curb." The other police officer, Roberts, stared at her with an unreadable expression.

She continued to plead and beg. "You have to believe me. Those aren't my drugs. Please take them off the roof of your car."

"I will ask you again to comply," the officer said. "Please take a seat on the curb."

Kelli sat. Still sobbing, she crossed her arms over her knees and dropped her head. She took deep, shaking breaths, trying to calm herself.

She says, "I obviously had trouble complying with their request to sit and be quiet, but I felt like I was in the fight of my life. I'm a mother and wife and caretaker of children. I had all these people who depended on me. I couldn't let them down. I had to prove my innocence."

As she sat on the curb and tried to compose herself, she kept picturing how she must look to the parents driving by—those parents who entrusted her with their kids. She felt like one of those suspects in a cop TV show. She felt like those bad people who'd broken the law, even though she was innocent.

*My God, Sydnie can't see me like this.*

Her thoughts raced. When would she wake up from this nightmare? She pinched herself hard to make sure this was really happening. *Ouch!* It hurt. No, this wasn't a nightmare. Not in the traditional sense, at least. She was awake. Wide awake, existing in a different kind of nightmare. This was real life, with parents driving by gawking, administrators gathered in the parking lot to see what the commotion was about, and children staring dumbfounded. Kelli could read the expressions: *Why are the cops talking to Miss Kelli? Is she being arrested? What did she do?*

Tears flowed down her face. She was sobbing so hard it was difficult to catch her breath.

She could see the accusatory expressions already: people wondering what she'd done, parents trying to reconcile the Kelli they knew with this woman being interrogated by law enforcement.

*"Maybe we don't really know her."*

*"What did she do?"*

*"She clearly broke the law."*

*"Cops don't just show up like this for no reason. She had to have done something wrong."*

That assumption—that she must have done *something* wrong to bring this on herself—would follow Kelli for years.

The drugs were still there, on top of the police car for the world to see. Time felt as though it had slowed down. How long had those drugs been up there on the roof? Minutes? Hours?

Somewhere nearby, Sydnie was wondering where her mother was. She was going to be scared when her mom wasn't there waiting for her. She was only ten. She might come looking for Kelli.

*Syd can't see this. She can't see her mother like this.*

Kelli clenched her hands together. Her heart raced so hard in her chest she was afraid she might be on the verge of a heart attack. Her knees trembled, knocking into each other. Her teeth chattered in her head. She felt close to vomiting. Her thoughts raced together in her head, fragments running together like a bleeding watercolor painting.

*Watercolor. Are they supposed to do watercolors in the afterschool class today? No, Syd is doing cartooning.* For a nonsensical moment, Kelli wondered if she could just get up, walk back to the classroom, and go back to her normal day. Go back to her normal life…a happy, simple life where she could help her daughter and classmates paint with watercolors or do cartooning.

Simple pleasures like that now seemed so far away, so unreachable.

"Those aren't my drugs," she repeated again, as if by saying it enough times the officers would have to believe her and let her go. After all, this was America. Innocent people weren't arrested and tried, were they?

Well, yes, sometimes they were. Even in a country that had the best technology and resources, mistakes were made. Stories of false arrests and imprisonments made the news. Was she going to be one of those falsely arrested and imprisoned people? It seemed not only possible, but likely.

"The drugs were in my car. I had no excuse," Kelli says. "All I had was the truth."

She closed her eyes and tried to find internal strength. But all she felt was fear. Her chest squeezed tight. She bit her lip to keep it from trembling.

*This can't be happening.*

The thought that she might be arrested at that moment, handcuffed and thrown into a police car in front of her colleagues, students, and daughter, was enough to cause her to burst out wailing again. She couldn't help herself. Deep, primal sobs left her throat. Loud, guttural cries. Embarrassing sobs, but she couldn't stop them. There was so much at stake at that moment: her daughter's view of her, her school reputation, the image in the schoolchildren's minds. What would Sydnie's peers think? Her daughter's friends? She'd known so many of them since they were toddlers. Kelli had seen them grow up. She'd been involved in their lives. She couldn't stomach the thought of those children thinking she was now a bad person, a criminal. Not to mention that if she went to jail, what would that mean for Sydnie? Would she lose custody of her? She knew enough from the DARE program at school that having pills on school grounds, which looked like intent to sell, was a felony. And felons often lost custody of their children.

It was too much to think about, too much to process. She was in a horror show, too terrifying for words.

"Please take the drugs off the roof," she repeated once again. "The kids are going to see them, and they'll think differently of me. I don't want this impression in their minds. My daughter is here. She can't see this. Please."

The officers didn't respond to her pleas. To them, they were dealing with a probable criminal. The evidence was right there, undeniable. There were drugs in bags, plain as day. They'd heard it all before. Seen it all, too. People often appeared different on the outside from who they really were. Yes, this woman looked like a law-abiding citizen, a typical suburban housewife, even if she had a bit of a free spirit about her and a peace sign on the back of her car. But years of working the beat had taught them that even in Irvine, all was not what it seemed. In this case, it seemed pretty cut and dried. There had been a call, and they had found drugs. Simple as that.

The cops continued to pepper Kelli with questions:

"Do you do drugs?"

"Absolutely not," Kelli said.

"Do you know anyone who does drugs?"

"No."

"Did you have someone in your care who does drugs?"

"No!"

"How old is your daughter?"

"Ten."

"Does she do drugs?"

"Oh my God, no! She's *ten*."

"Do any of her friends do drugs?"

"No way!"

"Does your husband do drugs?"

"Never."

"Are you having marital problems?"

"No way, my marriage is good," Kelli said. "We're a very mellow

## "I'll Get You!"

couple. We don't fight. We're nice to each other. We really love our life."

"You sure he wouldn't leave drugs in your car?"

"No way! First of all, he doesn't do drugs. Second, he loves me and our daughter. There is no way he has a hand in this."

"Any friends in the car recently?"

"No, only children."

"How old were they?"

"Six years old. Little kids." Kelli racked her brain for how this could have happened. *Did I leave my car door unlocked?* "Those drugs must've been planted. They're not mine."

"Who would plant these on you?" Officer Shaver.

"I don't know. I don't know," Kelli said, trying to catch her breath. *Who would do such a thing?*

"Do you have any enemies?" he asked.

She thought for a moment. As it began to dawn on her, her chest squeezed tight. "Actually, yes. I do have an enemy." Kelli wasn't one to immediately accuse someone of wrong doing, which was why she hadn't immediately thought of Jill Easter in relation to this strange occurrence. Her mind just didn't work like that.

"What is this person's name?" Officer Shaver asked, holding a pen to his notepad.

Kelli swallowed hard. The year of harassment she'd endured flashed through her mind in rapid-fire bursts. *Jill Easter.* Of course.

So the torment wasn't over after all. The reprieve that Kelli had welcomed had all been an illusion.

"Do you know your enemy's name?" Officer Shaver asked again, watching her intently.

"Yes," Kelli said. She clasped her damp hands together. "Jill Easter."

A deep horror seeped through her veins, like a slow-building noxious cloud. She stared at the officer through her tears. *Could it be?*

*Could Jill Easter really have done something so evil?*

It not only seemed possible, but likely.

Everything faded out for a moment and then slowly faded back in. Kelli gripped her forehead, nausea building. Her breaths came out in short, rapid puffs. *Am I hyperventilating?* She felt like a deer in the crosshairs with no way out.

*I'll get you!* Those words rang in Kelli's ears. Everything blurred and began to close in on her. At that moment, she was struck with the horrifying sense that her life was changing right there, right before her eyes. Changing, mutating, like a monster in a bad sci-fi movie.

She had the heightened sense that her old life was disappearing right in front of her—slipping through her fingers like sand—and that things would never be the same again.

Unfortunately, she was right.

That moment changed everything.

Nothing would ever be the same again.

# ten

While parents and bystanders continued to gawk, Kelli sat on the curb outside Plaza Vista Elementary School and tried to answer the police questions as best she could.

She knew she looked like a common criminal. She felt like one, too, but all she could think about was Sydnie and how worried she was going to be when she got out of class to find her mom not there. In all the years of raising Syd, Kelli had never once not shown up.

"I need to go to my daughter," Kelli said to Officer Shaver. "She'll be getting out of class soon, and I need to let her know I'm okay. She's going to be worried about me."

"All right," Officer Shaver said. "We'll escort you to your daughter."

He and his partner accompanied Kelli across school grounds. People stared, mouths agape, to see the popular school volunteer flanked by all-business law enforcement and marched through the halls. She caught the look of disappointment in the DARE officer's eyes when she passed.

"It devastated me," Kelli says.

From then on, she hung her head as if guilty, afraid to meet the eyes that followed her. She couldn't bear to see the accusation in their expressions or the doubt about her character.

Sydnie was standing outside her classroom, her young face etched with worry and fear. When she saw her mom escorted up by the police, her eyes widened and her mouth fell open. Tears immediately filled her eyes. She rushed to her mom, sobbing.

"Are you okay? What's happening?" she asked.

Kelli drew her daughter into her arms. "It's okay, Syd. It's all a misunderstanding." She pulled back to look into her daughter's eyes. "Listen to me. It's going to be okay. Please don't worry. I just need to talk to the police for a while and get it cleared up."

"But what happened? Did you do something wrong?"

"No," Kelli said, her throat pinched tight. "I did nothing wrong. It's all a terrible mistake. I'll get it fixed soon. Just sit here and wait for your dad. He'll be here soon."

Officer Shaver stepped forward to address Sydnie. His tone was kind and gentle. "I'll need you to go sit down and wait for your mom, okay?"

Sydnie nodded.

An administrator standing nearby touched Kelli's arm. "I've called Bill for you," she whispered. "He'll be here soon for Sydnie."

Kelli nodded gratefully, biting her lip hard to hold back the tears. She didn't want Syd to see her cry. Her daughter was so frightened already.

The police officers escorted Kelli into a nearby conference room.

"It was all windows," she says, "so everyone was able to look in and see me getting questioned."

Officer Shaver and his partner, Officer Roberts, put Kelli through a lengthy field sobriety test. They had her say her ABCs both forward and in reverse. They asked her to touch her nose. They asked her to open her mouth so they could look inside. They shined a light into her eyes. All of this while people—colleagues and parents and children—watched outside.

She came up negative on all tests.

When it was over, she prayed that the police would finally let her go. She was shaking from stress and humiliation.

"May we search your house?" Officer Shaver then asked.

"Why?" she said.

"It's part of the process, ma'am," he replied. "It's standard procedure."

"No way," Kelli said. "I just want to go home with my family." She'd had enough and felt so invaded. She couldn't stomach the thought of the police—strange men she didn't know—going through all of her personal items at home. She just wanted to go home to her safe life and sleep this nightmare away.

Plus, she was innocent! Why did she have to submit to any more of this? It felt so unjust.

The officers gave her a studied look that said volumes. She realized what their expressions meant. If she didn't let them search, she seemed guilty.

"I immediately wised up," Kelli says. "I decided to let them search so they could see that I had nothing to hide. There were no drugs in my house or anything that resembled paraphernalia. I just wanted to get this over with and clear myself as a suspect."

By that time, Bill had arrived. He'd gone immediately to Sydnie to make sure she was okay. When the police learned that he'd arrived, they asked him to join his wife in the conference room. They then started questioning him as well.

Sydnie sat outside and watched her parents through the window as the cops in uniforms stood over them. Her face was streaked with tears.

After a while, the police asked to follow Kelli and Bill to their apartment. Sydnie went with her father to his car while the police escorted Kelli to her PT Cruiser.

As Kelli drove home, she gripped the steering wheel so tightly that her knuckles turned white. She looked in the rearview mirror to see the police car tailing close behind. Behind the police vehicle was Bill's car with Sydnie inside.

*What must Sydnie be thinking?* Kelli's eyes smarted with tears. She could only imagine how frightened and confused her ten-year-old girl must be to see her mom driving up ahead followed by scary-looking police cars.

"The thought devastated me," Kelli says. "Up until now, Sydnie had lived a very innocent, sheltered life. I wanted her to have a joyful childhood. I'd protected her from as much negativity as I could. To her, cops only followed bad people who'd done something wrong. I couldn't bear the thought of her seeing me—her mom—that way."

The caravan arrived at Kelli's apartment building.

"It was so embarrassing and scary," Kelli remembers. "I pulled into my complex with the police close behind me, and they parked right out front. I can only imagine what the neighbors were thinking. I thought maybe the cops would arrest me now that my daughter and husband were home. I wasn't sure what was going to happen next."

Instead of arresting her, the police officers escorted Kelli up the stairs to her apartment while her husband and daughter trailed behind.

"Please stay here in the entryway," Officer Shaver instructed Kelli, Bill, and Sydnie. Then the police entered the apartment.

*Oh my God, what if Jill Easter also planted drugs in my apartment?*

"I couldn't watch," Kelli says. "I just turned my back. I could hear them move from room to room, opening drawers and cabinets and the back sliding glass door to the patio. I remember my dog losing his mind and barking, which made things worse. It was a very different and threatening kind of situation that none of us had ever experienced in our lives."

Kelli, Bill, and Sydnie stood in the entryway, holding tightly to each other's hands.

Officer Shaver passed by and said, "I need to know where you keep your baggies."

"My baggies?"

"Little clear sandwich bags."

"Oh. In the second drawer down next to the dishwasher."

"Okay." He disappeared into the kitchen, and Kelli could hear him rifling through the drawer.

Outside, it started to sprinkle. Earlier, it had been an unseasonably warm day, and now it was drizzling. The dismal weather matched Kelli's mood.

After a while, both the police officers approached her.

"We're finished here," Officer Shaver said. "We've called a crime scene investigation team. They're going to come out to collect evidence tomorrow. They'll take fingerprints and DNA off your car. They will also be taking DNA from you and your family."

Kelli's first thought was, *Oh no! The rain is going to wash away any possible DNA evidence or fingerprints of the suspects who committed this crime.* She'd had such foul luck all day, and now this.

"Do understand that you are not to leave?" Officer Shaver said.

Kelli nodded, unable to formulate words. She couldn't believe that the CSI were now involved.

"This was the kind of stuff you only see on TV," she says. "It completely blew my mind. I just kept nodding my head and complying with their requests, but inside, I was dying. I felt so bad for Bill and Syd. I knew this was making them sick. Syd was so frightened. She couldn't stop crying. Bill was trying so hard to be strong and not react. We were holding on to each other's hands so tightly. I didn't want to ever let go. Ever. The whole time, I thought I was going to be handcuffed and taken away from my family."

Every time Officer Shaver's police radio went off and he would respond, Kelli thought he was being instructed to arrest her.

"I was in constant fear," she says. "I was shaking, praying, begging God to save me. I was so scared."

Later, during the court trials, Officer Shaver was asked why he didn't arrest Kelli that day. He replied that her behavior and answers were that of an innocent person. He'd been on the force for a long time and had seen it all. His experience and judgment said that Kelli was telling the truth.

"Obviously, he didn't know for sure," Kelli says, "but whatever I did and said was enough to keep me out of handcuffs and jail. I was innocent, so I was acting innocent, and Officer Shaver somehow knew. I'm not stupid; I knew innocent people went to jail every day and then had to sort it out there: get a lawyer, get arraigned, and post bail. I was lucky."

When the police left, Kelli closed the door and turned back to her family. She was unable to stop the torrent of emotions that washed over her.

"The police were finally gone, and we were left to sort it all out," she says. "I started to cry and couldn't stop. I sobbed uncontrollably for hours. Bill and Syd just sat on the couch and watched me cry."

When she'd finally purged her shock and fear, she looked around her dark apartment and realized how late it was.

"We didn't know what to do," she says. "We were all in shock. We didn't eat dinner because none of us were hungry. Instead, we locked all the doors and windows, turned on all the lights in the apartment, grabbed the dogs, and just huddled together in the bedroom until morning."

Bill and Syd finally fell into a restless sleep, but Kelli didn't.

"I didn't sleep a wink that night," she says. "Instead, I watched my family sleep. I kept apologizing to them as they dozed. I was so sorry this had happened. This was too much for them. They both looked so frazzled, not peaceful at all. Just completely worked over. I knew that my life had just changed, and that I would need to start making arrangements for my family. I could go to prison at any moment, and I needed to prepare. I had so much to do."

"I'll Get You!"

The next morning, Kelli pulled herself out of bed and tiptoed out of the room so her family could continue to rest.

"I decided to keep Syd home from school that day," she says. "I also called a friend to cover my volunteer shift so I could stay home, too." With no sleep, the thought of going to school and facing people made Kelli feel ill. That sensation—of feeling physically sick—would become a regular part of her life after that.

She sat on her couch and began calling her closest friends and family to tell them what had happened. In the event she might be arrested and taken to jail, she felt she needed to make arrangements for Sydnie.

"I called my brothers and dad and asked for their help in picking Sydnie up from school. They would all have to take turns according to their schedules," she says.

Then she received her first phone call from the detective assigned to her case, Detective Andreozzi.

"He was straightforward and very serious," Kelli says, "and at the time, also very scary."

The detective began the long, detailed process of investigating Kelli and her family. He was pursuing any and all leads. He told her he would be calling her frequently with questions as the investigation continued, and to expect constant phone calls.

Bill awoke and came into the living room. He told Kelli he would be taking the day off work. He was too worried about Kelli and Sydnie to leave them alone.

"We were under the impression that we were in a lot of trouble," Kelli says. "Also, we felt incredible danger from Jill Easter because we knew she was the one who'd done this evil thing. It showed how imbalanced she was, how unpredictable, and how downright frightening."

Kelli also continued to worry that the police would come at any minute to arrest her. The rest of her day was spent on high alert, filled with uneasiness. Every time she heard a distant siren, she was sure the police were coming for her. Every time the phone rang, it was either the detective with another set of questions, or the school, or friends and family inundating her with questions.

"I felt completely out of control," Kelli says. "My stomach was in knots every time the phone rang. It was nerve-racking."

Soon, the CSI team rolled into the parking lot in a huge white truck with blue lettering. The officers, dressed in uniforms and wearing gloves, surrounded Kelli's car and began going over every square inch of her vehicle. They opened the glove box and checked under the seats. They took swabs and samples. They examined every nook and cranny. They wrote notes and conferred with each other. They milled about the car and Kelli's apartment, looking for evidence.

"That giant CSI truck was quite the event at my apartment building that day," Kelli says. "All of my neighbors and friends saw. It was the beginning of the whispers and speculation throughout my neighborhood."

The CSI team then took DNA swabs from Kelli and Sydnie. Kelli's heart ached to see her little girl holding her mouth open for officers to swab inside her cheeks. Syd looked stricken. Her eyes were wide with fear, and she was trembling.

"Am I under suspicion too, Mommy?" she asked.

"No, honey, they just have to do this as part of their investigation."

But no matter how much Kelli tried to reassure Syd, she couldn't erase the look of terror in her daughter's eyes.

Kelli began mentally preparing herself to be led away in handcuffs in front of Syd, which felt as though it could happen at any moment. She needed to be strong for her daughter. No matter how frightened she was, no matter how anxious and upset, she couldn't let Sydnie see her break down.

After the CSI team left, Kelli prepared lunch for her family, but none of them could eat.

"That would be the first time I threw up my food," Kelli says. "It started happening all the time after that."

The principal of the school, and Kelli's supervisor of the ACE program, called frequently throughout the day to check up on her.

For the rest of the day, Kelli found herself going around to all her windows and doors to make sure they were locked. She also kept constantly looking out the windows.

Sydnie was terrified, too. She was afraid to go into her room. If she had to get something, she would run into her bedroom, and then run out quickly as she could, completely out of breath. She started begging Kelli and Bill to go with her.

"She was only ten when the drugs were planted," Kelli says, "and she felt as though Jill could be hiding in her room, waiting to kidnap her. To Sydnie, Jill was the Easter Monster. There wasn't anything we could do to make her feel better."

That night, Kelli didn't sleep again. She lay awake all night, watching her husband and daughter doze. She kept going through all of the events in her mind, as if constantly replaying them would help her make sense of what had happened.

Four days passed. On Sunday night, Kelli's nerves were on high alert at the thought of going to school on Monday. She didn't know if she could handle seeing the questioning faces, the doubt, or Jill's smug face. The police had said they would escort her to school, which gave her a small amount of comfort. There were undercover officers who were to be positioned at the school to investigate all leads.

Somehow, Kelli found a small flicker of determination inside her. Even though she was exhausted from five nights of no sleep, she got out of bed that Monday. She got dressed, made breakfast, and got Bill off to work, just as she always did. Then it was time to take Syd to school.

Kelli received a text from the detectives who would be escorting her to school. They were downstairs.

Kelli and Syd exited the apartment and saw the unmarked car in the parking lot, parked next to Kelli's PT Cruiser.

The detectives, both dressed in jeans and collared shirts—with visible gun belts—greeted her.

"We will be following you," one of the detectives said. "We want you to take the same route that you always take to school."

Kelli and Syd drove to school with the unmarked car following them. When Kelli and Syd arrived at school, the detectives parked and then escorted them to the office.

"Go about your day," one of them said. "If you see Jill or Layton Easter, stay away from them. Don't go near Layton's classroom. Don't talk to either the mother or the child. Do your regular things. And if you see us, don't say anything. Don't talk to anyone about us. Pretend we're not here."

Syd went to her class, and Kelli returned home. Later, when she returned to volunteer at the ACE program, she became aware of the whispers. They were more pronounced than they had ever been. Whereas before, not everyone had believed Jill's gossip, now it seemed as though everyone was convinced that Kelli was guilty.

"Only my friends and staff treated me normally," Kelli says. "Everyone else acted like I was a criminal. It was terrible."

Jill, for her part, avoided Kelli. She no longer made eye contact or stood around gossiping and pointing at Kelli. She seemed to go about her daily life without a care in the world.

"She had a satisfied little smile on her lips," Kelli says. "Here she'd planted drugs on me, and yet she just went about her business. I was blown away by her nonchalant, cavalier attitude."

While Kelli went about her days at Plaza Vista, the police were working hard on their investigation.

"After two months, I was finally cleared," Kelli says, "but instead of being able to shout it from the rooftops as I wanted, I had to

*"I'll Get You!"*

remain silent. The police were actively gathering evidence on the Easters after that, and I couldn't do anything to jeopardize the investigation. So I had to let people continue to think I was guilty."

As for Jill Easter, she continued to avoid Kelli at school or make eye contact. However, something hadn't changed. Jill continued to show up at places where Kelli frequented.

"Orange County is a large place," Kelli says. "With more than three million residents, it seemed odd that Jill Easter would often happen to be in the same place as me, at the same time."

One time, Jill pulled up next to Kelli at a stoplight, looked over, and started laughing. When she pulled away, Kelli burst into tears.

"It might seem silly to get so worked up over a bully," Kelli says. "But it was so much more than that. The fact that she'd planted the drugs took it to a whole new level. I felt she was a threat, and she had the attitude that she was going to get away with whatever she did to me. The police later confirmed that I was in danger, so my instincts were right. But at that time, it was difficult to explain to people why I was reacting so extremely to her ridiculous behavior."

Everywhere Kelli went, she looked over her shoulder. When she would spot Jill, her heart would drop and she would have an immediate physical reaction.

"She was everywhere," Kelli said. "It was obvious she was watching me. She even told an administrator that she was going to hide in the bushes and make sure I was following the ACE rules. I would see her all over town. It was upsetting that she was going about her business like nothing happened. I would see her at Costco, the pool, the grocery store, parades, just acting like normal. She and Kent would be laughing and shopping while I was a complete mess. Every time I saw them somewhere, I would start to have a panic attack and have to leave."

At night, Kelli's nightmares increased. She began having recurrent dreams of Jill hiding in the bushes, and then jumping out and slitting her throat.

Even holidays weren't immune to Jill and Kent's harassment.

"I saw them at the Newport Beach Christmas Boat parade," Kelli says, "and they were standing behind us on purpose as if to taunt me. I felt a chill, turned around, saw them, and adrenaline kicked in. I thought they were there to kill me. I immediately grabbed my family and we left. There had to be ten thousand people there at the parade that night. How did the Easters find me? It was no coincidence that they showed up all the time wherever my family and I were. I'm sure it happened more than I knew. I caught them several times, but what about all the times I didn't see them? Being at the boat parade and knowing they were lurking in the dark behind me…it was absolutely terrifying. All I could think about was Jill coming up behind me and slitting my throat. In all the madness and thousands of people, I felt she would get away with killing me and leave my child motherless. I also thought at any moment that they would grab my daughter. I held on to Sydnie so tightly. I had to leave the parade with my family. I hate them for that. They knew what they were doing. They were terrorizing us, terrorizing my child. They were the boogeymen. It was creepy; they were stalkers. Dangerous people. I kept thinking, *When are they going to arrest her?* I just couldn't take much more. She was everywhere, and I felt like I was going to die."

At school, people continued to avoid Kelli. Every day, more friends dropped off. Parents who used to say hi now turned their heads.

"I could see that I was very much guilty in their eyes," Kelli says. "I'm sure they were wondering why I was being allowed to continue with my duties. Sometimes I just wanted to quit and stay home and fade away, but something inside of me wanted to prove all of the haters wrong. In fact, I wanted to take on even more responsibility at the school. I wanted to prove the doubters wrong."

Meanwhile, the police were busy investigating all leads. At first,

## "I'll Get You!"

Jill Easter wasn't at the top of their suspect list, despite Kelli's certainty that Jill had everything to do with the drug planting. After all, the caller had been a male, and Kent Easter had had no previous interaction with Kelli.

Instead, the police focused on another suspect, a mentally ill parent from Plaza Vista who'd wanted to take Kelli's PTA position as president. He liked to run around the school wearing a Batman outfit. The police were familiar with him due to many previous complaints for his odd and questionable behavior. In one such instance, he painted the word "Security" on the side of his car, and then parked out front of the school to film parents and their children in order to "catch them running stop signs." (He was later arrested for pretending to be a security guard at a local high school and pulling out a gun on campus. The police were called, and he went to jail.)

The police soon cleared the Batman-costume-wearing suspect due to a concrete alibi. Detective Andreozzi then turned his attention to tracking down the identity of the anonymous caller who had reported Kelli for "suspicious driving."

There were a few leads to go on. The caller was a local male and had an apparent Indian accent. He'd given a phone number and address that both turned out to be fake. The Irvine Police smelled a rat, and assigned many officers to the case. Their first priority? Find out where the phone call had originated.

What they would eventually uncover would change the direction of the case forever. Not only that, but Kelli's worst fears would be confirmed.

In the meantime, though, things continued to get worse for Kelli and her family.

# eleven

After the drug planting, a year passed. Kelli's life and that of her family's was still being affected by the actions of Jill and Kent Easter.

Kelli was called often by Detective Andreozzi and the district attorney prosecuting the Easters, Chris Duff, to keep her updated on the investigation.

"I was naturally curious as to how it was going," Kelli says. "But the DA and detective always kept our conversations brief. I knew they were making progress on the case, but I didn't know how much. We didn't know when or if the Easters would ever be arrested. We were constantly having to think about it and deal with it. It was stressful."

Kelli could also see that she was still very much guilty in the eyes of many people at the school.

"I'm sure they were wondering why I was been allowed to continue with my duties," she says. "Sometimes I just wanted to quit and stay home and fade away, but something inside me wanted to prove all of the haters wrong. In fact, I wanted to take on even more responsibility at the school. I wanted to prove the doubters wrong."

Kelli continued to get hate mail. When she walked her dog, people in passing cars would honk at her. She didn't know if they were honking to say hello or to yell something nasty to her.

*"I'll Get You!"*

"People knew who I was," Kelli says. "It was scary, especially because I didn't know their intentions. There was so much hate directed at me. I knew I was innocent, and my family and friends knew the whole thing was BS, but Jill and Kent were attorneys and influential and out to get me. After the drug planting, a lot of people started to believe them."

After all, physical evidence had been found in her car. She'd been detained by the police. No one had been arrested yet. Although Kelli had been cleared, but no one knew that. To outside observers, it appeared that the outlandish accusations thrown at her by Jill Easter might be true after all. After all, why would someone go to those lengths to frame a person like Kelli? Who would do that? Why would someone go to such effort? It seemed unfathomable to most people.

The stress began to affect Kelli's family more acutely. Kelli's former glossy, thick hair was falling out in even bigger clumps, so much so that she considered getting a wig. She continued to lose weight and sleep, and her nightmares increased in frequency. Her daughter's anxiety returned. Syd had been slowly regaining her confidence again during the reprieve from the Easters, but after the drugs were planted and the gossip resumed, she reverted to the withdrawn shadow of a little girl she'd become.

Bill, who'd always been the rock of the family, began to have panic attacks. All the years of persecution, questioning, ostracizing, and seeing his family in pain had taken its toll.

His insomnia increased. His hands trembled when he tried to drink his coffee. It became increasingly difficult for him to function or work. The man who had been so full of life, so vibrant and strong, the man who used to get up at the crack of dawn to go surf before work, was a shell of the man he used to be. He no longer rushed in from work with boundless energy, only to grab Kelli and Sydnie twirl them around in bear hugs. He no longer smiled or laughed or cracked jokes. He became gaunt and thin. He had no more zeal for life. He began to fade. He sat for hours on the couch, staring at his computer, trying to focus on work but unable to. His job began to suffer, and he was no longer able to drum up business like he had when he was able to concentrate. Kelli became so alarmed that she asked him to see a psychologist, which he did.

Dr. Nina Rodd diagnosed him with major depressive disorder at moderate or severe level.

Bill was struggling, and watching his suffering filled Kelli with torment.

Once again, it appeared Jill and Kent Easter had won.

"If they wanted to hurt me," Kelli said, "then they succeeded. They harmed me in the worst possible way that another human being can hurt someone: by hurting the ones I loved."

Even school wasn't a reprieve for Kelli anymore. The dirty looks, the gossip, the whispers: all of it escalated. She became known as "the chick with the drugs in her car." People actively speculated about the foolishness of the school for keeping her on. The principal and the Irvine School District continued to support Kelli, but they were constantly having to defend their decision. Anyone involved was not allowed to talk about the investigation.

"Let the wheels of justice do their part," the principal told Kelli. "The truth will prevail."

But time seemed to drag on at an excruciating pace.

"Try living a year with everyone thinking you're guilty of something you didn't do," Kelli says. "People make judgments and treat you differently. It was hell. The worse part was seeing Sydnie's and Bill's demise, right before my eyes. I didn't know when it would end."

Kelli's phone continued to ring off the hook. Friends and family called constantly to check up on Kelli and hear the latest details of the investigation.

"Everyone wanted to talk about what was happening," Kelli says. "They wanted to discuss their points of view and their concerns. On the one hand, I love that everyone cared so much. I understood and appreciated their help. But on the other hand, all I did, all day long, was discuss what was happening in my life. It just never stopped. I couldn't turn it off. Sydnie would put on her headphones and tune out and draw, and Bill would just sit on his computer and try to survive and make money. No one wanted to go out anymore. We were getting too much attention, both good and bad. Talking with my family and friends was completely therapeutic, but it went on for a year. I became burned out, and so did Bill and Sydnie. We wanted our lives back so badly. Things had changed so much. We weren't prepared for what was happening. Nobody could have ever prepared us for this."

One day, Kelli was working in the office and heard a commotion. All the administrators and teachers were abuzz. Someone ran up in to the office and said, "Kelli, look outside! There are reporters outside the school."

Kelli went out front with a few other teachers to investigate.

"We were all wondering what was happening," Kelli says. "I didn't think it had anything to do with me."

Then her cell phone rang. It was the DA, Chris Duff. She hadn't met him in person yet, but he'd talked to her daily by phone, updating her on the case pending against the Easters. Although she'd been intimidated by him at first, she now considered him a friend and ally. He'd taken a special interest in her case, and, as a truly good district attorney does, was determined to see justice on her behalf.

Instead of his usual calm, stoic voice, Chris sounded different this time. He sounded elated.

"I have good news, Kelli," he said.

Time slowed, and then seemed to stop. Kelli knew what he was going to say before he said it.

She held her breath.

Then Chris said the words she'd been waiting so long to hear: "Jill and Kent Easter have been arrested."

A rush of emotion hit Kelli like a tsunami. For a long moment, she couldn't speak. "The feeling that came over me can only be described as intense," she says. "Extreme emotion."

Her whole body began to shake. It was difficult to breathe. When she finally gathered herself, she screamed into the phone, "Oh my God! Thank you. Thank you!" Tears streamed down her face.

After two years of hell, two full years of struggle and harassment and sadness and loss, there would finally be justice. There would finally be an end to her ordeal.

"There's still a lot to do," the DA said. "I'll call you later." He paused. "Congratulations, Kelli. We did it! Go celebrate."

"I can't thank you enough." Kelli hung up. Electricity coursed through her body. She ran down the halls of the school, screaming, "They got arrested! Jill and Kent Easter were arrested!" She hugged everyone in sight, tears streaming down her face. "I'm innocent. I've been cleared! They were *arrested*!"

People hugged her. The administrators, the people who had stood by her for so long, blinked back tears.

"The press outside is for you!" someone told her.

"The press?" Kelli blinked in confusion. Why would the press be outside to see her? Had this made *the news*?

She couldn't believe that the news of this ordeal had reached the media, and that the story was of interest to people. After all, she was just a simple person, a regular mom and homemaker and PTA member. She wasn't different than any other hardworking woman in America.

What she didn't realize was that her ordinariness, that "regular person" aspect, was one of the reasons why her story so captured people. If a woman like Jill Easter could fixate on a simple person like Kelli Peters—a woman just trying to get by and live a decent life and care for her family, friends, and community—it could happen to anyone.

"At the time, I didn't understand how big this had become," Kelli says. "I was completely blown away by all the attention. All I wanted to do was scream to the world that I'd been cleared. The DNA evidence showed the truth. The Easters had been arrested! They were guilty, not me! The amount of pressure I've been under for so long had finally exploded: the taking the high road, the keeping quiet, the talking to no one…all of it had finally been set free. I could do and say whatever I wanted. I could scream to the world, 'I told you, everyone! I'm innocent!'"

Kelli peeked outside the school to see a multitude of news vans parked outside. Reporters hovered about, waiting for a chance to talk to her.

Her! Kelli Peters, regular person.

It was surreal.

Kelli immediately called her closest friend, Dina. "Come to the school as quickly as possible!" she said in a rush, barely able to formulate the words. "I need a ride. My car is surrounded by the press. I don't know what to do."

Kelli's infamous vanilla PT Cruiser with the peace sign sticker on the back window was hard to miss. When Kelli poked her head around the building, she could see the press milling about her car and talking to people in the parking lot. Reporters were stopping parents in their cars and interviewing anyone they could. Parents were there to pick up their children, only to be accosted by a gaggle of reporters sticking cameras and mics in their faces and barking questions at them.

"Everyone looked confused and stunned," Kelli remembers. "It was crazy! I wondered what people were thinking about all the commotion, or what they were saying to the reporters. I couldn't believe all this was centered on me."

The principal approached Kelli and said, "Come back to the office and wait for your ride. You can hide out there."

Inside the principal's office, Kelli called her husband and texted all of her family members, friends, and dog park group to tell them the good news. They were ecstatic.

"Watch the news," Kelli told them. "Reporters from channels 2, 4, 5, 7, and 11 are all out front of the school."

As Kelli talked to each of her friends in the safety of the principal's office—her beloved principal who'd supported her and stood by her all this time—she got a lump in her throat. She was grateful for the support of those who'd believed in her.

"I couldn't have made it without them," she says. "Through all of the destruction caused by Jill Easter, I saw the goodness in people. I saw and felt the love. It surrounded and buffered me. Amidst all of the pain, all of the suffering and hatred and evil actions directed at me by a crazy woman for no reason, I saw the good around me more clearly than I'd ever seen it. That's the irony."

Dina, one of Kelli's most loyal supporters and a friend who'd never doubted her for one moment, came running into the office.

She enveloped Kelli in a tight hug. They stood like that for a long moment, with no words, only emotion between them. They drew back and looked at each other.

"You did it," Dina whispered to her friend. Tears filled her eyes. "You did it, Kelli."

Kelli's heart swelled with gratitude. It was people like Dina who'd kept her going, kept her from dying beneath the horror of the past two years.

Kelli and Dina collected Sydnie, and then headed to the car. They got in quickly, before the news reporters could find them, and drove off.

"It was so funny," Kelli remembers. "It was as if I were some sort of important person. It felt crazy and bizarre. We were laughing about it the whole time. Rushing away with Dina in a 'getaway car' like that, pretending I was some sort of celebrity, was a moment of carefree fun, of celebration, after all the years of torment."

At a stoplight, Dina pulled up next to a news van.

"We ended up right next to Channel 9 news and the reporter Michelle Gile," Kelli says. "I motioned for her to roll down her window, and she poked her head out and said, 'Yes?' I asked her what all the commotion was about, knowing full well what it was for. She said, 'We're looking for Kelli Peters. Do you know her?'"

Kelli and Dina looked at each other and burst out laughing. "I'm Kelli Peters," Kelli blurted out.

The reporter looked stunned. "Can you pull over and chat with us? I promise it will be okay."

Kelli and Dina exchanged a glance, and then Kelli nodded. "Okay," she said, and Dina pulled over to the side of the road.

"I had no idea what to expect," Kelli says. "This was my first interaction with the media. I was already in high heaven from the news about the Easters being arrested. I felt as though nothing could ever go wrong again."

Michelle Gile began asking Kelli questions. Kelli immediately liked her and felt a connection with the reporter. Michelle not only seemed genuinely interested in the story, but in Kelli as a person. Her demeanor was kind and open. As an Irvine resident and PTA volunteer herself, Michelle related to the story.

"She made me feel so comfortable," Kelli says. "I was so happy to be finally telling my side of the story. And then my phone rang."

It was the DA. "How are you doing?" he asked. "Are you okay?"

"Yes," Kelli said, "but there's a ton of media outside the school."

"Don't talk to the media," he said.

Oops!

"Oh no!" Kelli said. "I'm talking to Michelle Gile from Channel 9 at this very moment."

"Hand her your phone," Chris said. "I need to speak to her."

Kelli dutifully passed her cell phone over to the reporter.

Michelle listened to the DA for a few moments, and then said, "Okay, I understand…but you owe me one!" She then handed the phone back to Kelli, disappointment on her face.

"We had to stop the interview," Kelli says, "but Michelle Gile still remains my favorite news reporter in the world. She was so kind and considerate. I will always be grateful for the classy way she handled my delicate situation and respected my situation. It was such a funny moment when we pulled up next to her. It was a great day. I feel like a dolphin who'd been trapped in a fishing net for years and finally released. I was happy, bubbly, jumping around, hugging everyone in my path. It was a day I will never forget."

When Kelli and Dina pulled up in front of Kelli's apartment building, there were several TV trucks already parked outside the complex. Kelli and Sydnie snuck past the reporters who were all clamoring out front, hoping to get an interview.

Kelli and Syd rushed up to her apartment. Just as Kelli was putting her keys in the door, she got another call on her cell phone. This time, it was from Channel 5 news.

"They were right outside," Kelli says. "I was so inexperienced. I didn't want to hurt anyone's feelings. I never once stopped to think, *How did all these people get my phone number and address?* It was so odd."

Kelli ran back down the stairs and saw a local reporter, Chip Yost, standing by the pool. She started giggling. *I know this guy! I've seen him on the news!*

Chip asked to talk to Kelli for a minute. Kelli bit her lip. She needed to buy time. She knew she wasn't supposed to talk to reporters, but she didn't want to be mean.

"I need to run upstairs and go to the bathroom," she said. "But I'll be right back."

She went upstairs, gathered herself, told Bill that there were reporters outside, giggled again because it seemed so outrageous, and then headed back down. When she approached Chip, she said, "I'm not supposed to do any interviews per the district attorney."

Chip said, "How are you doing?"

"I'm doing great," Kelli said. "This was that day I've been waiting for. It was a long time coming."

That sound bite ended up on television.

"I felt bad," Kelli says. "I knew I wasn't supposed to talk, but he asked how I was doing, and I wanted to answer him and not be rude. I saw that he'd probably been waiting for a long time, and I didn't want him to have to leave with nothing. In my mind, these people had families to feed, and they were just doing their job. I really didn't see the harm. He was a very nice reporter."

Kelli went back upstairs, turned on the television, and huddled up with her family on the couch to watch. As she waited for the news to come on, Kelli's heart raced. *Is this really happening?*

Then the news came on.

"Oh my God," Kelli says. "There I was! Big as day, on the screen. My face was on every channel. My phone was blowing up! Everyone saw me on TV. The news was getting out of the Easters' arrest, and it felt like the whole world was celebrating with me. What a day! I hadn't been sure that day would ever come. Besides getting married to Bill and giving birth to Sydnie, that was one of the best days of my life. The Easters would finally pay for what they did to me and my family."

From that moment on, Kelli's phone rang nonstop. She began fielding calls from all around the world. Every news station in every state and every country was calling her personal cell phone.

"It was," she says, "to say the least, *wow!* Overwhelming. My little story had taken on the longest legs."

In the days to follow, random strangers would come up to Kelli and tell her how much they related to her, or how this easily could have happened to them. There were so many aspects of her story that seem to be relatable to others.

"It really freaked people out to know that there were people out there that could take things this far," Kelli says. "I was so lucky that I did not get arrested. People were telling me how great our police department was. Jail would have killed me. The whole scenario of getting handcuffed and put in a police car in front of my neighbors, friends, and family would have ruined me. It would have devastated my daughter and my family, both mentally and financially. Officer Shaver, a brilliant police officer with years of experience, saved my life with his good judgment."

In the days and weeks that followed, Kelli tried to go about her daily life, but finally had to accept the fact that she was now a local celebrity.

"Every day was an adventure," she says. "I couldn't go anywhere without being recognized. People were coming up to me all the time in the grocery store and everywhere I went… People I knew, people I didn't know."

Eventually, all the attention began to wear on Kelli. The most difficult part was that Sydnie was having a hard time with all the focus on her mother and herself. When Kelli spoke to reporters, Syd would shy away from them and remove herself.

"Sydnie was completely bummed out by the media attention," Kelli says. "She was worried about her new school friends and what their reactions would be. She didn't want to lose friends again like she had before: friends she saw every day, went to concerts with, went to the beach with, and had built strong bonds with. She was terrified that it would all go away again in an instant, like it had before. On top of it all, she had to share her mom's time with the media. She'd been used to having me to herself, but all of a sudden I became a public figure. We couldn't go anywhere. Most people wanted to say hi and congratulate me, but there were a few who came up to apologize.

*"I'll Get You!"*

I'd gotten lots of hate mail from people who were very openly abusive, but some had been quietly pissed at me as they watched from the sidelines."

One of those people approached Kelli in the grocery store a short time after the arrest. A woman stopped Kelli and said, "I need your forgiveness."

"What do I need to forgive you for?" Kelli asked, her palms starting to sweat. Was this one of the people who'd sent hateful, abusive emails? Or was she one of the women who'd left threatening voicemails? Or one of the strangers who'd driven by and yelled obscenities at her and her child from their cars?

"I was Jill and Kent's friend," the woman said. "I was supposed to be with them on the night they planted the drugs on you."

"Oh?" Kelli asked, her throat tightening.

"Yes," the woman said. "The Easters had invited me and my family over so our kids could play together. Last minute, Jill canceled. My husband and I were later convinced that Jill Easter had wanted to use us as her alibi."

"I'm sorry to hear that," Kelli said. "I'm glad you didn't get together with her that night."

"I feel very guilty about believing all the lies that Jill Easter said about you," the woman said. "I've been to their house many times, and I was convinced that the story they were telling people about you was true. I thought you were a horrible person who hurt children. I believed everything they said about you, and I wanted to see you go down. When they got arrested, I was completely dumbfounded." The woman gazed at Kelli intently. "I am a religious woman. I need your forgiveness in order to move on. Will you grant me that?"

Kelli started to tremble. There was something about the woman that was off-putting and upsetting.

"Her vibe was stern and a bit pushy," Kelli says. "She was one of those people who had tortured me without knowing me. She knew she was wrong, but still, she'd done it. I didn't know how to respond. I had such mixed feelings. My family and I had been put through sheer hell for the past two years, and it hadn't been only because of Jill and Kent Easter. It had also been because of the people who'd jumped on the bandwagon and believed the lies and then took action against me. These people hurt me and my family to a depth they couldn't possibly understand."

Waves of pain washed over Kelli as she thought of her beaten-down daughter, the little girl who had suffered so much. She thought of Bill and how strong he'd been whenever she'd collapsed in his arms after another horrible email or call. She bit back tears as she recalled every moment of what she, Syd, and Bill had endured—a painful reel of memories in her heart and mind.

The woman continued, "Another thing. I don't believe Kent Easter is guilty. I know him. Jill might be, but Kent couldn't possibly have done what they're saying."

Kelli began to violently shake. "Kent is involved. They have him on video. They have evidence!" She couldn't believe this woman had approached her asking for forgiveness, and now was defending Kent to her face. This was the man who'd called the cops on her and started the whole chain of events. The last thing Kelli felt like doing at that moment was defending herself—*again*—to the naysayers, especially after all the evidence.

The religious woman crossed her arms and studied Kelli. "You're wrong about Kent," she stated. "It couldn't have been him."

At that point, Kelli couldn't have spoken even if she'd wanted to. She was too upset to pursue the conversation further. She'd been on a high for a few weeks, feeling as though her name had been cleared to the world. And yet there were still people who doubted. There were people who still didn't see the truth, or maybe didn't want to. Maybe there were those who never would, and to them she would always be that woman with the drugs who harmed children.

It hurt.

At that moment, Kelli felt so very alone. Sydnie wasn't with her like she usually was. Trips to the store now took two hours instead of twenty minutes because of all the people stopping Kelli, so Syd now opted to stay home instead. Even their old fun routine of going to the store together was gone.

Kelli was now trembling so badly that one of the store associates approached her.

"Are you okay?" the cashier, Isabella, asked.

Kelli shook her head. "No, I'm not."

Isabella put her arm around Kelli and escorted her away.

"I was really grateful to her for that," Kelli says. "She saw how much pain I was in talking to this woman, and how upset I was. I was crying because I was being forced to face one of the angry haters who was trying to apologize for herself, not me. I wasn't ready for this, and I wanted so badly to get away from her. The cashier, Isabella, saw this. She came up and got my arm and took me away. This is one example of how my friends protected me from the haters."

Weeks passed, and things began to calm down, but only slightly.

Although Kelli felt vindicated by the arrest, there was still much to be done. The DA was busy preparing the case against the Easters. Kelli was expected to give testimony on what she had endured.

The thought of facing Jill and Kent Easter in court twisted her stomach into knots. Kelli hated the thought of being up on the stand in front of a whole courtroom of people, refuting lie after lie told by two people who didn't know her. Kent Easter, in fact, had never met Kelli before in his life. Jill had met her once. From what Kelli knew, they'd hired the most high-powered and expensive attorneys in all of Orange County.

"Will we be able to beat them?" Kelli asked Chris. "What if the jury believes them instead of us?"

"Don't worry," he said. "The Irvine PD did a great job. We have enough evidence. I'm going to nail them. The truth will prevail."

Kelli tried to breathe a sigh of relief. She wanted so badly to believe that justice would win out, but she also knew not to take anything for granted. She knew who she was dealing with in the Easters. The rest of them—the attorneys, the media, the investigators—still had a lot to learn. It was up to her to tell them every detail of what she'd endured. Some of it was small and insidious, like how Jill Easter would stare her down with cold, dead eyes. Some of it was downright frightening, such as the stalking her everywhere she went and hiring people to spy on her. In order to help everyone convict the Easters, Kelli would have to relive it all again in minute detail. She didn't know if she had the emotional reserve to go through it.

"I had to find interior strength somehow," she says. "If I didn't, the Easters might win. So I had to gear up to experience every moment of pain all over again: the harassment, what it did to my daughter, what it did to my husband, having to leave the school and the PTA position I loved, the judgment, the threats, the terror, the illness, the loss of employment and income…all of it. I had a big fight ahead of me."

Kelli found it hard to believe that it had all come to this. What had started as an innocent misunderstanding had now led to two attorneys being arrested, and worldwide media attention. There were innocent children on both sides being hurt by Jill and Kent Easter's actions.

And for what?

Kelli still had a difficult time making sense of it all.

One of the worst parts was that Jill and Kent Easter still had it out for her. It was pretty clear that they weren't going away anytime soon. Who knew what kind of shenanigans they would pull in court to save face? Who knew what lengths they would go to continue to try to destroy her? They'd gone so far already.

Kelli's gut told her that she needed to be strong for what was around the corner.

"I felt there was another phase of hell in store for me," she says.

Her instincts proved to be right.

"I would love to say that after Jill and Kent Easter were arrested, everything was over," Kelli says. "But unfortunately, things had just begun."

Soon, Kelli would be in a new fight for her life.

# twelve

The dramatic events between Jill Easter and Kelli Peters were the constant talk of Plaza Vista Elementary School. Of course, that eventually trickled down to the children. As often happens, the kids at Plaza Vista absorbed what was happening around them and responded in kind.

Unfortunately, one of the biggest casualties in Jill Easter's campaign of destruction was a child: Sydnie Peters.

Before any of the Jill Easter events happened, Sydnie was a happy child with lots of friends. She loved playing and being surrounded by other kids. Being social had always been an essential part of her personality, ever since she was a little girl. Other kids gravitated to her as much as she did to them.

"She was always so social," Kelli says. "For example, when she turned five years old, she wanted to have a pool party but had a hard time limiting the number of friends she wanted to invite. She knew so many kids and didn't want to leave anyone out. She wanted to invite all of her friends and classmates, plus their brothers and sisters, too. She was seriously haunted by the fact that she might hurt someone's feelings by not including them."

After trying to negotiate the numbers down, Kelli finally threw in the towel. "What the heck?" she says. "If Syd wanted a gigantic

## "I'll Get You!"

birthday bash where she excluded no one, who was I to say no?"

Kelli sent out an invitation to all of Sydnie's friends and classmates and their siblings…a hundred children total.

Kelli asked her three brothers to act as lifeguards for the event. She recruited her husband and her dad to be the barbecue chefs. She went to Costco and bought as many hot dogs, buns, chips, and drinks that the cart could handle.

Sydnie was insistent that nobody brought presents to her birthday party. Instead, being the animal lover that she was, she asked all of her friends to bring a donation to the local animal shelter instead.

"Sydnie was so excited to design the invitation," Kelli says. "We attached a flyer with all the things the animal shelter needed: bags or cans of food, toys for cats or dogs, gently used blankets and towels, cash donations. You can imagine how much stuff we collected for the shelter the day of Syd's party. She was overjoyed. All she wanted to do was help the animals."

Sydnie's party was a huge success. Everyone swam, played pool games, ate hot dogs, listened to music, and had cake. At the end, Sydnie passed out little goody bags of candy to take home.

When the party was over, Sydnie helped her uncles load up a truck with all of the donations for the animal shelter.

The workers at the animal shelter were shocked when Syd and her family arrived with all of the donations in tow.

"You should have seen the looks in their eyes when we backed up the truck to the shelter's storage area," Kelli says. "Sydnie was beaming with pride and joy. She was so proud that she'd given up birthday presents in order to donate all of these amazing things to helpless, underprivileged animals. She insisted on doing this for her birthday every year after that, and we were happy to do it for her. I was so proud of her. She was such a happy child, with such a big heart."

Sydnie loved school. From the day she first started at Plaza Vista, she ran straight to her classroom, as fast as she could, eager and overjoyed to be there.

"Plaza Vista was such a great school," Kelli says. "We loved the idea of Sydnie being able to attend from kindergarten through eighth grade with all the kids she'd grown up with. Our dream was for her to go there all the way through, and then start high school with all the kids she'd grown up with. There was such a family atmosphere at Plaza Vista. The kids were great, and it was wonderful for Sydnie to see her same teachers every day. It felt so cozy and safe. Everyone was nice and happy. Life was good for Sydnie for the first four and a half years of school at Plaza Vista. She had the same friends year after year, and made new ones along the way. There were many different nationalities at the school, and it was so cool and interesting to meet the kids and their families from different countries or cultures. It was a very unique place, and we loved it."

All of that changed after Jill Easter set her sights on Kelli Peters.

At first, Sydnie's friends and peers started asking her questions about why people thought her mom had hurt Jill Easter's son and deliberately locked him out. Sydnie tried to explain that those were all lies, but the kids began to treat her differently.

On the playground, some of Sydnie's old friends started to distance themselves from her. Then the children started to choose Syd last for games or activities. Some children stopped talking to her, then more. Soon, no one was playing with her at all.

"She became invisible," Kelli says. "Before that, she'd had more friends than anyone. She was always the one to bring in any outsiders or ostracized kids, the ones with no friends. And now, she was that person. Except this time, there was no one to bring her in to the group or be her friend."

Sydnie began eating lunch alone every day. Her former ebullient confidence fell. It became hard for her to concentrate, and her grades dropped. She became quiet and withdrawn.

"Those kids were so mean to her," Kelli says. "Everyone used to like her, but now she felt as though everyone thought she was weird. It made her self-conscious. I watched her playing by herself and sitting by herself, and it killed me. She had her head down, with the saddest look on her face. She would watch all of the kids playing without her."

Sydnie became preoccupied and withdrawn. She started forgetting things. One day, she forgot to bring a red pen that her fifth grade English teacher required.

"She could barely face the teacher to ask to borrow one," Kelli says. "She was so ostracized that it made her painfully shy. She used to be so outgoing before. The teacher, not knowing the turmoil Sydnie was going through, scolded Syd in front of the class and made an example of her. Sydnie took it so hard that, to this day, she tears up when she talks about it. It was just a simple, forgetful mistake, but to Sydnie, it was too much to be pointed out and scolded in front of kids who no longer liked her. Because she'd lost all her friends, she had no one to turn to for support. She felt completely alone."

One time, Sydnie was eating lunch alone again on the playground. She saw a large group of children playing where it appeared there was no limit to the number of kids who could play. She decided to muster her courage to join in. She put down her sandwich, got up, and approached the group. Before, she would have been instantly welcomed into the group. But instead, when she walked up, the kids frowned at her. A boy looked at her and said, "Go away. There's no room for you."

That was the last time Sydnie tried to play with anyone after that. She'd gotten the message. She played by herself from then on.

Every time Kelli saw her daughter by herself, she remembered the happy, lively, outgoing child that Sydnie had been before Jill Easter entered their lives…and Kelli would cry.

"It was excruciating," she says. "I've never felt such pain in my life." She began asking her friends to have their children play with Sydnie.

"The kids would for a short time," Kelli said, "but it was forced. They would awkwardly try to play with Syd, but they didn't want to be bullied themselves. So they faded away, too."

Sydnie asked her mom to not ask kids to play with her anymore.

"She felt like people felt sorry for her," Kelli says. "It was embarrassing. She'd become such an outcast. Before any of this happened, she was the happiest kid. It was so sad to see her that way."

One incident Kelli witnessed drove a knife through her heart. It was during the "Fifth Grade Olympic Games" that the kids played at lunch. The children were all picked for teams, but no one wanted Sydnie. They either ignored her or told her to go away. She stood there by herself, an abject and lonely little figure, as all of the kids walked off with their teams.

"Sydnie was so upset that she started crying," Kelli says. "I mentioned it to a teacher, but she'd been too busy to see it happen. I wasn't supposed to step in because kids needed to work things out for themselves, but Sydnie was left behind and no one noticed. She was crying, but everyone was too busy to care. It was fifth grade, and I wasn't supposed to get involved, but I had to speak up for her. Nobody did anything to make sure she was included or to ensure that it wouldn't happen again. I was so upset and angry, but I had to keep it inside. So did Sydnie. I've never forgotten that day. It changed something inside Sydnie and me. We both grew a sadness we'd never had before."

Kelli started taking Sydnie off campus for lunch so her daughter wouldn't have to eat alone. "I would pick her up and take her out from that day on. She would cry while we ate our lunch. She didn't understand why the friends who'd loved her had suddenly gone away. It was hard to explain any of it to a ten-year-old girl who'd done nothing wrong. She was so tortured and lonely." Kelli blinks back tears as she remembers. "If I had it to do over, I would have taken her out right then and there and moved her to a new school. But the principal and administrators were trying desperately to help her. They kept trying to come up with strategies to make things better. None of it worked. Looking back, it was already too late. The damage was done. Sydnie had lost all her friends. She was being scapegoated and bullied. She would never be the same again."

Kelli even considered homeschooling her daughter, but she didn't have the emotional reserves. She was using every ounce of energy to survive Jill Easter's campaign of psychological warfare.

"I kept hoping things would get better," she says. "But they never did. Sixth grade was even worse. Jill had planted the drugs on me by that time, and people were treating me and Syd like lepers. I don't blame the kids, though. It was the parents' responsibility to teach their children to be kind."

One day, Sydnie approached her mom and asked to change schools.

"At first, this devastated me," Kelli says. "This was the school we'd been at from the beginning. We knew everyone. The principal, teachers, and administrators loved us and had our backs. I was president of the PTA, volunteering in a position that I loved more than any job I'd ever had, even though I didn't get paid. I'd been nominated for PTA president again and would have to find someone to fill my position. Sydnie had known her classmates since kindergarten. Plaza Vista was our family. I couldn't imagine leaving."

When Kelli looked into her daughter's face, though, the decision was clear. It was the right decision to leave. Sydnie's happiness came first.

"Most kids don't want to leave their friends," Kelli says, "especially ones they've known their whole lives. But that was it. There were no more friends."

Kelli immediately sprang into action. She drove to a nearby

school called Lakeside and talked to the administrators. They were warm and welcoming. They also had a place for Sydnie.

Kelli drove home and told her daughter that her wish would be coming true. Sydnie would be going to a new school for seventh grade.

She was ecstatic. She cried and thanked her mom.

When Kelli broke the news to the principal of Plaza Vista and the other administrators, they were heartbroken. "Don't go," they begged her. "You've been part of this family since the beginning. You're an integral part of the school. You're PTA president. We need you! If you go, Jill Easter will have won."

"I've made up my mind," Kelli said. She had tears in her eyes. "I need to do what's right for Sydnie. I can't see her suffer any longer."

The principal, teachers, and administrators all wished her and Syd well. The whole office was crying when she left.

"Yes, some people might say that Jill Easter won," Kelli says. "She got what she wanted. She got rid of us. But I never would have let her run us off if I hadn't seen what it was doing to Sydnie. Jill got me where it hurt the most…my daughter. My love for her trumped everything else. I made the decision and never looked back. Sydnie and I walked away from a school and a community that we loved and had been part of since she was little. But none of it mattered anymore. Sydnie's wellbeing came first."

Although leaving Plaza Vista was painful for both Kelli and Sydnie, it turned out to be the right decision. Sydnie was happy at Lakeside. She immediately made friends and was welcomed into the school.

"Finally, things got better for Sydnie," Kelli says. "There was no more ridicule, torment, 'no, you can't play here,' hardship, or pain. She was finally back to her happy self again, and that gave my heart so much peace."

Unfortunately for Kelli, though, her own torment was far from over.

Jill and Kent Easter were not done with her.

It would be a long time before Kelli would find any peace of her own.

# thirteen

*From Sydnie Peters, who was aged ten when the Easters planted drugs on her mother (she is sixteen now):*

"I never understood why no one at school liked me after Jill Easter started spreading lies about my mom. It felt like it happened in one second. Everyone who was my friend before was suddenly gone. It was like I was a nuisance, like I was just taking up space. No one would notice if I left. When I did eventually leave to change schools, I was right. No one noticed.

Sixth grade was humiliating. I started school with no friends because of what had happened to my mom. I was put into Project Success, a program for kids with special problems. They really wanted me to be in this group, but I felt so out of place. It was counseling, but no one really understood what I was going through. I would be pulled out of class, and my schedule was completely changed. It took up a lot of my time, even my lunch. I was so alienated, even while in that group. It felt like they were removing me from the general population because I didn't fit in. I didn't fit in anywhere, so hey, put me in permanent counseling! I think the school was trying to protect me but all they did was draw more attention to me. I'd had so many friends before, but now I was so lonely and sad all the time. I started a

## "I'll Get You!"

class called cartooning with my sixth grade teacher, Mrs. Harvey. I couldn't wait for that class because I loved to draw. I started hanging out with a girl who lived by me and we did a lot of things together, but I think I was too stressed to keep friends. I started feeling like people thought I was weird. I knew I was probably a little weird before, but I didn't care because I had friends who liked me. After the incident when my friends started to leave me, I figured I was just too weird for the kids to handle. Besides being weird, now I became very sensitive. I would eat lunch alone and then walk around the track by myself. I would completely ignore the school and start pretending I was somewhere else.

My mom got me a sketchbook to take to school so that I could just draw during lunch, and I loved it. I was finally able to draw my feelings. I started to draw cartoons and make-believe stories. My mom was always trying to help me get through it, keeping my mind busy and happy. She continued to take me to lunch and make me feel good about myself. I remember a girl named Shreya who always tried to be my friend, but I was so far removed from everything by this time that I couldn't accept her kindness. I feel bad to this day for not becoming friends with her. She was so nice and amazing. She helped me one day when a bunch of kids ganged up on me and I was on the ground with my hands over my head trying to get away. I heard someone yelling, 'Leave her alone!' and when I looked up, it was Shreya. She helped me get up, and I was so shocked that she was there, on my side, helping me. I will never forget that day that she stood up for me. I wish I could have been a better friend to her. I hope she reads this and knows how much I appreciate her, and I hope she understands why I wasn't able to be her friend. I had decided that I couldn't allow myself to have any more friends because I got so hurt. I'm sorry I didn't trust her; I know now what a good person she is. I see her in high school every once in a while and have nothing but good feelings when she passes by. She was the one and only kid who ever stood up for me and secretly and silently stood by my side, all those years. Thank you, Shreya.

The day of the drug planting, the ladies at the desk told me that my mom was in the principal's office with the police. I was terrified. I thought something happened to my dad, so I started crying. I also wondered if I'd done something wrong. I remember hearing the word *drugs*. I was so scared. I knew my mom didn't do drugs, so what was going on? The ladies told me to sit down, and I just remember crying. I was hearing all kinds of things in the office. But then I heard talk of drugs in the car, and I was just trying to listen and figure out what was happening. My dad showed up, which made me feel better, but then the police took him in with my mom and started talking to him. I was so confused. I thought something really bad must have happened. Everyone looked so serious. The police asked Dad lots of questions. They were in there a long time. Janice and Beverly (from the office) were trying to make me feel better, but I was so upset.

The cops then came to search our house. They were kind to me, but I kept thinking that they were being way too nice. I thought they were being sneaky, like on TV where they pretend they are your friend and then they arrest you if you say the wrong thing. I didn't want anyone to say the wrong thing. I thought that if they tried to take my mom away, I was going to really fight to keep her home. I thought, *I'm going to grab her and run away with her, so that they can't take her.* I knew she was innocent, but I was afraid they were going to trick us by acting nice and then take my mom away. I was so scared.

When the police left, I didn't want to leave my mom's side. We all went in the bedroom, and Mom tried to calm me down. The police said they were coming back in the morning, and I was afraid they were going to arrest Mom then. The CSI police came the next morning. They were different people, and they took our DNA, which was really scary. I didn't go to school the next day. I just stayed with Mom and Dad and hoped and prayed nothing bad was going to happen.

The CSI team made me feel like it was okay, but they wanted to take my DNA with a swab. I felt that maybe my mom might be in more trouble than I thought because of the DNA. I thought she might get arrested. I was trying to trust the CSI team that they wouldn't touch her or take her, but I was ready to fight them. I would do anything to keep my mom from going away. I knew she was innocent. I would never let my mom go without a fight. I was ready to defend my mom. I told myself I would reason with them. I would do anything to save her. I was saying, 'Please check the DNA first. Don't take my mom!' If they tried to take her, I planned to grab my mom and hold on. They would have to take me, too.

Going back to school after that was so scary. I had no friends now, so I felt very scared. Mom was there all the time, so at least I had her.

My mom did a great job shielding me from what had happened. All I knew was there was a mean lady involved who had targeted my mom for no reason.

One girl who lived by us started to hang out with me a little bit. We both had dogs, so she would come over with her little dog and hang out. I think I was too nervous because of all the stuff that was happening, and eventually she stopped coming over. As things went on, a lot of people started talking about what had happened, and we were getting a lot of phone calls from TV shows and newspapers. I didn't like all the attention. Every time we went to the store, my mom got so much attention. She was always crying. I decided that I didn't want to go out any more, so I stayed home a lot. I started to draw even more.

One day I decided I wanted to change schools. I couldn't take being alone any more. I wanted to go somewhere where no one knew me. I knew that no one would notice that I was gone. No one cared enough. I just wanted to disappear.

I was lying in my mom's bed, and I had to get up the courage to talk to her about it. It was hard because we'd been at Plaza Vista since I was five years old. I finally got my guts up and said, 'Mom, can I move schools?'

My mom was shocked. I was crying. I knew I couldn't go back to that school next year. I was thinking about all the friends who I'd lost. All those friends whom I'd had for so many years, they didn't acknowledge me anymore.

I just wanted to have friends.

Mom said she would look into it. When she told me that I would be going to a new school in seventh grade, I felt like a new person. I couldn't wait! I was ready to be a new person.

On the first day of Lakeside, my new school, I was so nervous. I was immediately accepted into a group with the most popular girls. I never felt like I fit in even though they were so nice to me. One day, I walked with a girlfriend over to a group of kids that were acting completely goofy. I was instantly interested in them. They would be the best thing that ever happened to me. I felt like the other group would never miss me; after all, I was used to being anonymous. Later, I would find out that they did miss me and wondered what had happened. There was still a lot going on at home, but at least I had my new friends. They were awesome. My mom was so happy about my new friends that she took us everywhere. We went *everywhere*!

But I was worried about all the media attention. I didn't like it at all. I didn't want my new friends to know who I was. If my new friends found out, I might lose them.

I went to court once. I had to listen to the other attorney for Kent ramble about my mom and how bad she was. He said bad words, and underlined them up on a screen. He was vulgar and should have toned it down. I was just a child. I was so glad my dad and my grandpa were there. It was hard to watch my mom be upset.

When mom told me that Kent was found guilty, I was so relieved. I was even more relieved that Jill was in jail. I was very afraid of Jill. I called her the Easter Monster. I'd stopped sleeping in my room after the drugs were planted. There was a person stalking me and my family, and I was afraid of being kidnapped. I was afraid Jill Easter would take me hostage. We (my mom, dad, and me) all slept together for years after that. We watched cartoons and laughed. For some reason, my mom and I would get the giggles every night, every single night. It was such a good time and such a good memory during a very hard time.

I dove into video games during this time because it was a good way for me to escape. I wanted to play games and go on the internet, and I became a part of a kid's internet art group. Whenever my mom was talking to the press, which made me so uncomfortable, I was online with my art group or taking art lessons at an online art school. It's all I did. My mom did everything she could to shield me from the press.

The toll that all of this took on me was that I lost confidence and friends and trust. Now I'm very private. I don't want people coming over. I have barriers. I love my friends, but I don't want anyone over. I'm still a little worried about being judged. I wish I could have people over, like I did in the old days. But I've spent a lot of time alone now, and I like myself. I thought for years there was something wrong with me, but I was by myself a lot, and now I like myself. I'm very confident now. I'm weird, but I like my kind of weird. I was never 'mean weird.' I was just weird. I tried to change who I was, and then I became depressed. I just didn't know what to do. I tried to do other things. I started to figure out what I liked to do and that was drawing. Plus, I met some girls who were just as weird as me, and they were so cool, in my eyes…the coolest girls I've ever met! I trust them, and even though we went our separate ways in high school, I still love them and think of them as my friends. I know we will be friends forever. I'm so grateful for their friendship. I have a lot of good friends now. I have a special friend, Emilie, who totally gets me.

She and I get together, and it's like we speak the same language. She doesn't pressure me. She is so cool. We will always be friends, even if we don't see each other every day. I feel so lucky to have my friends. I'm lucky to have my family: my grandpa and grandmas, my uncles and my aunts, my cousins, my mom and dad. I know that I'm okay because of my friends and family. I've grown up a lot, and I'm happy now. I feel safe, and I hope my mom and dad will be okay. We will take care of each other always. We are strong and lucky to have such great people in our lives. The police, the attorneys who helped us, and Mom and Dad's friends. A lot of people stood by us, and it's a good feeling."

–Sydnie Peters

# fourteen

Now that Jill and Kent Easter had been arrested, things began to move along quickly. The Easters were charged with conspiracy to procure a false arrest, false imprisonment, and conspiracy to falsely report a crime. The district attorney, Chris Duff, was busy preparing Kelli's case.

"I met Chris in person for the first time before the grand jury trial," Kelli says. "Before that, I'd only spoken to him by phone. I obviously wasn't used to having conversations with DAs. It was unnerving."

In the beginning, Kelli's heart rate would pick up every time she saw Chris's number light up on her phone. She still feared that she could be arrested, so picking up the phone whenever he called was difficult.

"I only knew about DAs from watching TV," Kelli says. "I pictured a serious, busy office with powerful people. Mr. Duff was professional, but also very compassionate. After a while, he started to warm up to me, and that was nice, because I was always so stressed out. This whole thing was so out of my comfort zone. Mr. Duff couldn't talk too much about the case with me; it was very important we just stick to the facts. But after I met him for the first time, I absolutely loved him. He was so comforting and kind. I was always sick to my stomach, and he instantly made me feel better."

In person, Chris was serious and professional. He was a hardworking man of integrity who took his job as county prosecutor seriously. His success had come for good reason. He was devoted to his job and the victims for whom he sought justice, and his passion showed.

He'd gone to USC undergrad and then law school right after. He'd decided on law school with the intention of working for the FBI, which fascinated him. During law school, he participated in "ride alongs" with the LAPD during the 1992 Los Angeles riots, along with interning with the Bureau of Alcohol, Tobacco, Firearms and Explosives (ATF), which regulates federal violations. After law school, there was a delay in the FBI hiring him, so instead he interviewed with the Los Angeles district attorney's office. He was immediately hired. After working there for a while, he then received a letter from the FBI offering him a job, but by that time, he enjoyed working at the DA's office so much that he decided to stay. In 1999, he was hired as deputy DA of Orange County, where he has worked ever since.

In Orange County, Chris first worked the misdemeanors unit, then the gang unit, where he handled gang cases and murders. One significant murder stood out. An eighteen-year-old boy was at the wrong place at the wrong time: a party where gang members were present. The boy wasn't a gang member himself. He was the son of two LAPD detectives. There was a confrontation at the party, and the gang members slit the young man's throat.

"That case really stayed with me," Chris says. "It was such a sad waste of youth and potential. The parents were devastated."

In prosecuting the case, Chris became close to the victim's parents.

After winning the case, where the main defendant was given fifteen years to life, Chris felt a great sense of victory in bringing some semblance of justice to the grieving parents.

"I'm still close to them this day," he says. "We get together every year for a golf tournament benefit that they have in honor of their son. We also get together periodically for lunch to catch up on each other's lives."

A tough-as-nails, whip-smart prosecutor with a heart was just what Kelli Peters needed. She got that in Chris Duff.

"He cared from the beginning," she says. "He really wanted to see me get justice. I felt that strongly from him, just as I had from the Irvine Police Department. I was extremely lucky to have such bright, focused people on my side. For all of my bad luck in this case, such as being at the wrong place at the wrong time in encountering Jill Easter, I've also been very fortunate. There were some really good people working on this case for me."

After the gang unit, Chris moved to the special prosecutions unit, which handled high-profile cases involving the media, politicians, and cases against lawyers. When he arrived at the special prosecutions unit, the case against Jill and Kent Easter was waiting to be filed. The police had submitted their report to the district attorney's office, and this would be the first case in the unit that Chris Duff would handle. He read through the report to see if it needed to be filed based on the evidence.

"Everything was there," Chris says. "The DNA evidence, the cell phone records, video of Kent Easter going into the hotel to make the bogus phone call, etc. Irvine PD had assigned twenty detectives to this case. They were supercops and compiled a huge amount of evidence. They wanted to see justice. The fact that the Easters had used the cops to try and frame Kelli Peters did not sit well with them. Also, she was framed in their city of Irvine. Attorneys also took this case personally because Jill and Kent Easter gave all lawyers a bad name. Everyone involved wanted to see justice in this case."

Chris read the file and was convinced that both Jill and Kent Easter had conspired to frame Kelli Peters.

"Jill was the driving factor," he says. "But it didn't mean that Kent didn't play an active part in it all."

He immediately filed the case, and a warrant for arrest was put in the system so the cops could go apprehend the Easters.

"It was crucial to all parties involved that Jill and Kent Easter were arrested and put through the same legal and criminal process that they wanted Kelli Peters, an innocent victim, to go through," Chris says.

After Jill and Kent Easter were arraigned in court, the charges were read against them. They were then entitled to a preliminary hearing, which was to make sure that there was probable cause to show they committed the crime. Because the case had already taken so long to go through the system, Chris decided to take the case to the closed grand jury instead. That also served the purpose of keeping Kelli, in her fragile state, out of the hands of opposing counsel.

Chris called Kelli to tell her about this. "You'll need to testify in front of the grand jury," he said.

"What does that mean?" she asked.

"You'll need to get up in front of a jury of civilians and tell the truth about what happened to you. They'll make a decision on whether or not there is enough evidence to indict the Easters and set a date for trial."

Kelli was worried about her big day. On the morning of her testimony, she got dressed in a professional beige dress, applied waterproof mascara, since she knew she would cry, and took a deep breath. Today, everything rode on her shoulders. If the Easters didn't get indicted, then Kelli would forever be seen as guilty in the eyes of the world. There was so much at stake. Would she make a misstep? Say something that could hurt her case or give the Easters a leg up? She needed to be a good witness and speak articulately about what had happened, or there was a chance the grand jury wouldn't see the case for what it was. She couldn't take the chance of letting the Easters off the hook.

*"I'll Get You!"*

*You got this, Kelli*, she told herself as she smoothed her hair and straightened her dress. *You'll be okay. Stay strong.*

The drive to the courthouse was nerve-racking. Every stoplight felt like hours. As Bill drove, Kelli sat stiffly in the passenger seat, looking out the window. Her chest was tight with anxious flutters. She didn't know what to expect. The process felt so daunting, so *official*. Jill and Kent Easter were familiar with courtrooms and the legal process, but not Kelli. The unknown was the scariest part of all.

Luckily, she knew she was in good hands with the DA. He would guide her through the process, as would his assistant, Rick Bradley.

"Rick was a badass," Kelli says. "He helped me so much."

Kelli was thankful to have such a dedicated individuals at the DA's office on her side. She couldn't imagine going through this ordeal with a distant or removed prosecutor or some checked-out attorney just punching the clock on his job.

Still, even despite the support, her nerves increased when she arrived at the courthouse.

"My spirit was so low," Kelli says. "I had little hope. Everything felt daunting. We'd just sat in horrible traffic to get there. I didn't know if I was dressed right. We couldn't find parking. There were homeless people camped out and sleeping on the ground. There was a skinny, stray cat that I wanted to feed. I saw lines of potential jurors with pissed-off faces pulling out their belongings for metal detectors, and cops watching them with stern faces. The courthouse was a cold, beige, brick building. It looked like a friggin' prison minus the wire. Inside, I had to sit on a hard wood bench outside the DA's office, which is all glass and metal. There were no flowers or color…there was nothing cheerful about the DA's office! Everything felt so hopeless and bleak to me at that moment. And then I saw Chris Duff."

Chris walked through the DA's office doors to greet Kelli and Bill. He was immaculately dressed and had a giant smile on his face.

He immediately approached Kelli and gave her a hug. He shook Bill's hand.

"Are you read to go get 'em, Kelli?" he asked.

"No," she said. "I'm scared."

"Don't worry, you got this, Kelli," he said, the same words she'd said to herself earlier. "Just go in and tell the truth. Just be you. And smile, for God's sake!"

Kelli couldn't help but give him what he wanted. "He was such a ray of sunshine, so cheerful and ready to go kick butt. I couldn't help but smile at his positive energy. It was like an electrical charge to my spirit. It instantly snapped me out of my mood and brought me back to my senses. I felt like things were going to get better."

Kelli, Chris, and Bill walked down the long hall past offices where people were behind their desks, working hard. Kelli was still feeling apprehensive, but that all changed when she entered the conference room where she would wait to be called before the grand jury. She blinked in surprise to see a room filled with everyone who had ever been involved with her case. The room buzzed with positive energy.

Kelli recognized Officer Shaver, Officer Ayala, Detective Andreozzi (who was holding a book of the evidence—the "discovery"—as if his life depended on it), Kelli's victim advocate, Katie Zabinski, who'd always been a phone call away, and the CSI team who had investigated her…just to name a few. Chris also introduced her to the 911 operator, the forensic scientist, and the employees from the Island Hotel where Kent had been caught on video before making the police call about Kelli.

Everyone said hi and greeted Kelli and Bill.

"I was blown away," Kelli says. "I couldn't believe all these people had shown up just for me. This was our team, and they were here to make things right on my behalf."

As she held Bill's hand, a lump formed in Kelli's throat. She looked around at all these caring professionals who had worked so hard on her case, and she felt a rush of gratitude. Tears began to trickle down her face.

"Everyone from the beginning to the end of my ordeal was there," Kelli says. "They all played a major role in bringing this case to the grand jury. My entire team was in that room sitting around the table. It was a beautiful moment…a moment when I felt a synergy with all these people who had helped me. There was such a deep connection there. Everyone was excited and upbeat. They were all happy to be there, ready to present their findings and testify. Each person in that room held a vital piece to the puzzle. At that moment, I felt lifted up by them all, and it was then that I knew I could do what needed to be done. I was going to testify with everything that I had. Everyone had worked so hard for me. I wasn't going to let them down."

Soon, Kelli and Chris were called to the grand jury room. Bill gave Kelli a kiss.

"Good luck, honey," he said. "Don't be nervous."

Kelli entered the courtroom and took a seat in front of the jurors. The jury was made up of a group of regular people whose sole job was to weigh the information to see if there was enough evidence to indict Jill and Kent Easter. The jurors were seated around a giant square desk. Kelli took a seat at the head. A court reporter sat off to the side, poised and ready to transcribe the proceeding.

With a dull headache beginning around her temples, Kelli looked at the jury's faces staring back at her. They were all studying her. Some were serious looking, some had blank expressions, and some were smiling graciously. Her life was in their hands. She knew that grand juries didn't always indict defendants if they didn't feel there was enough evidence in a case. She hoped with all her heart that they would see the facts for what they were.

Chris started by giving instructions to the grand jurors. Then, one by one, they started asking Kelli questions. Kelli answered each inquiry the best she could.

"I could tell that some of them were disturbed by my story," she says. "I started to cry at one point. Mr. Duff was very attentive. He stopped the questioning so that I could recover."

Chris asked, "Are you okay to go on?"

"Yes," Kelli said, taking a deep breath. "Let's get this done."

For a few hours, Kelli did her best to explain and clarify the details of what had happened to her.

"It was difficult to go back over everything," she says, "but I persevered until it was over."

When she finished testifying, she went back into the conference room where the rest of her team waited for their turns.

"When I saw them again, I realized how very important that roomful of people was," Kelli says, "and I thanked them all from the bottom of my heart."

She turned to Chris Duff and said, "You're amazing. Thank you for saving me. Thank you for helping me and my family."

Later, Chris called Kelli to tell her that the grand jury had indicted Jill and Kent Easter.

"All the stress was worth it," Kelli says. "When Mr. Duff called me to give me the news, I was so happy. From that moment on, I was excited to get calls from him. He was on my team. He became like my family, and he still is."

Chris's passion for the case, and his determination to win, gave Kelli the strength that she needed.

The date for the criminal trial was set for October 2013, and Kelli geared up to face her nemesis in person.

On the eve of the trial, the day before going to court, Jill Easter pled guilty. She was sentenced to 120 days with no home confinement.

She was going to jail.

The fact that she'd been sentenced to serve time in the county jail was important, as sometimes wealthy people who committed nonviolent crimes were allowed to serve house arrest.

Jill's children were allowed to visit her in the Orange County Jail, but she was required to serve her term straight through.

"It was symbolically important that she went to jail," Chris Duff says. "She was a rich Orange County housewife who'd committed a serious crime, and people wanted to make sure she paid for what she'd done. It meant a lot to Kelli that she was sentenced and had to do jail time."

Chris felt that by Jill pleading guilty, it was a defense strategy to take the blame in order to save Kent Easter's bar card so he could still practice as an attorney.

"I felt strongly that the Easters planned to have Jill plead guilty in order to try to save Kent's income," Chris says. "They would paint him as the hapless, duped husband and hope that the jury would let him off. Then he could still continue to practice law and support Jill and their children. However, it didn't matter if the whole defense strategy was to 'blame Jill,' because we knew that both of them were accomplices in this crime. We weren't going to let Kent get away with his part in it."

Kelli says, "Kent had been an excellent attorney who was trained in what was right and wrong. He knew the consequences for committing a crime like this, so it was extra important that we get him."

For Kelli, she was not only glad that Jill went straight to jail, but that she would not have to face the Easter Monster in court.

"The last thing I wanted to see was her self-satisfied, cruel face glaring at me as she told lie after lie," Kelli says. "To me, it would be like looking into the eyes of the devil."

Although Kelli would not be dealing with Jill Easter at the criminal trial, she would still have to contend with Kent. To that date, she had never met him. She didn't even know what he looked like. This was a man who'd taken an active part in trying to destroy her life, and he'd never even laid eyes on Kelli before.

"I'd never even Googled him," Kelli says. "I didn't want to know what he looked like. Kent pretended that he didn't know what he'd done to me, but he knew full well. He was an active participant in planting the drugs, and he made that phone call that started the whole thing. He'd never even met me, and yet he didn't care about what he was doing to me. To this day, he has never shown any remorse. Kent Easter is as devoid of conscience as his wife. How those two ever found each other, God only knows. But when you put two people with zero consciences together and they justify their actions to get what they want, this is what you get."

As the date of the trial got closer, the DA helped Kelli prepare. She was a ball of nerves and could hardly sit still. In the days leading up to the trial, she didn't sleep. Nor did Chris Duff, for that matter.

"Not many prosecutors sleep during their big trials," Chris says. "I spent every moment going over the case in my mind, strategizing, preparing, and getting ready to tell the story to the jurors. I didn't want to overlook one detail."

The morning of the trial, Kelli internally geared up for the fight of her life.

"I can't remember a time when I was more afraid than going into the criminal trial," Kelli says. "Not only would I see Kent Easter in the flesh, but Jill was supposed to testify, too. I would have to tell my story from beginning to end, and it would take days. I knew Mr. Duff would be easy and gentle with the way he handled my testimony. But I was terrified of the Easters and their pit-bull attorney."

Soon, the trial was underway. Chris had prepared a detailed case. He was ready.

When Kelli walked into the courtroom for the first time and saw Kent Easter sitting before the judge, her chest pinched with anxiety. He looked so smug, so emotionally devoid. He was wearing an expensive-looking suit and flashy watch, and his hair was gelled back.

He looked like a man of wealth and power. His attorney looked the same. They seemed ready to do battle, which unnerved Kelli.

"They both looked very intimidating," Kelli says. "Kent's attorney was well known for defending crooks, and I was warned that he would be tough. I felt very small, and my courage diminished a bit at the thought of being in the same room with them for that period of time."

Luckily, whenever Kelli felt weak, Chris was there to pull her back up.

"I always felt like I was with the number one attorney in the room," Kelli says. "Chris Duff was so smart and bigger than life when he was working the courtroom. He was in his element, and as a seasoned pro, he knew what he was doing. His strength gave me strength."

Courtroom proceedings began, and soon it became clear what the defense strategy was on the behalf of Kent Easter:

- Depict Kent as a beaten-down, cuckolded husband whose wife was having an affair. He supposedly did everything she asked without question.
- On the night of the drug-planting incident, Jill had Kent's cell phone because hers had a bad battery. She was up late that night, taking care of her sick child, and then went out and planted the drugs without Kent's knowledge.
- Jill woke up the next morning and called Kent at work to convince him to call the police on Kelli because Jill saw Kelli with the drugs.
- Believing his wife, Kent called the police.

Chris Duff went on to refute every part of the defense strategy. During the trial, he showed that Kent was not the "beaten-down husband" the defense claimed, but instead an active participant in the crime. Chris studied the cell phone evidence and discovered that Jill's phone was pinging by Kelli's house for eight straight hours the night of the crime, along with Kent's, which meant both of the Easters were co-conspirators in the crime.

"There was no disputing the cell phone evidence," Chris says. "It showed clearly that Jill and Kent Easter were both driving around Kelli's apartment the entire night before the drugs were found in her vehicle."

Days turned into weeks during the trial as witnesses were called, evidence was presented, and the attorneys presented their cases before the jury.

During the trial, Kelli learned many things about the investigation that she hadn't known before. One chilling thing she discovered was that after Jill had stayed up all night to plant the drugs, she'd parked and watched Kelli leave that morning to drive to school.

"She stalked me the entire time to make sure the crime went down the way she'd planned," Kelli says. "Who does that? She's the mother of three young children, and yet this is how she spends her time? She went to these great lengths to frame an innocent person whom she didn't even have a legitimate beef with. It was so creepy…so frightening."

An odd moment in trial was when the defense presented "evidence" trying to give Kent Easter an alibi. The attorney played video footage in court that showed Jill Easter supposedly caring for her sick child at 12:30 a.m. The camera then slowly panned over to Kent's cell phone sitting in the baby's crib.

"It was so obviously staged," Chris says. "Who gets up at 12:30 a.m. to film her daughter's cheek rash and then zoom in on her husband's phone? The data on the camera showed that the internal date stamp had been moved back to the night of the crime, so the video was fabricated by the Easters for a defense strategy. It was laughable. We said, 'These two are clearly trying to play us.' But it didn't work."

Another interesting moment in trial was when Kent testified about using his fake Indian name when he placed the call to the police. The jurors looked amused as they heard the recording of Kent's phone call, where he spoke normally at first but then changed midstream to a poorly done, exaggerated Indian accent.

During his testimony, Kent stated that he'd been genuinely worried about giving a fake name because he didn't want to get involved with framing Kelli. Instead of just stating that he'd made up a name, he instead said he used his Indian neighbor's name. Chris Duff investigated Kent's neighbors and discovered that Kent was lying. The name Kent had given the police during the bogus call was in fact a famous Indian-American movie actor, Jay Chandrasekhar, who starred in such movies as *Super Troopers*, *Jackass Number Two*, and *Beerfest*.

"I showed the jury that he was a liar," Chris says. "It was damning to him."

Trial antics aside, the most significant part of the case was that the Irvine Police Department had been able to trace Kent's phone call to the Island Hotel in Newport Beach. The Island Hotel employees went above and beyond to help. They discovered video footage of Kent entering the hotel right before the call was made. In his hand, Kent held a piece of paper that was presumed to be his script. The police took the photos back to Plaza Vista Elementary School, and people identified the man as Jill's husband.

"If the cops hadn't found the video," Chris says, "they wouldn't have been able to put the crime on the Easters. There was DNA evidence, such as the fingerprints found on the pills, but the investigators were only able to check it against known samples. Jill and Kent Easter weren't in the database. The police couldn't get a search warrant on Kelli's word alone."

Kelli agrees. "That video footage was key," she says. "If the police hadn't found that, the Easters never would have been arrested and tried. I would have been thought of as guilty forever."

Soon, it was Kelli's turn to testify. She took the stand and was asked a series of questions by the DA about the crime and the years of torment leading up to it. Then she was put through her paces by the defense attorney, who insinuated that her perspective of what she'd endured was overblown. He not only minimized what the Easters had done and its effect on Kelli, but continued to present Kent Easter as a spineless, hapless cuckold who had been controlled and duped by his cheating wife into committing a crime. The defense attorney repeatedly stated that Kelli wasn't falsely imprisoned.

"My whole strategy was to poke holes in that," Chris says. "I was irritated that the defense was going after Kelli like that. One of their angles was that Kelli wasn't falsely imprisoned. In fact, she was detained by the police in front of her workplace, her daughter, her friends and colleagues. She wasn't allowed to leave. If she'd tried to go, they would have cuffed her and taken her to jail. The defense said it was no big deal, though. They attacked her and minimized what had happened to her. This was a woman who was fragile to begin with, someone susceptible to something like this. If she'd gone to jail, it would have killed her. If I'd gone to jail for a crime I didn't commit, I would've been angry. But Kelli was emotional and easily broken. She was already traumatized from the Easters going after her, and now the defense attorney was attacking her. When they said she'd been 'free to go' all along, it angered me."

That defense tactic—of saying Kelli had been free to go when the police detained her at the school—so bothered Chris Duff that he got down on his knees in front of the jury to show what Kelli looked like when she was pleading with the cops to not arrest her.

"I re-enacted that moment where she was begging for her life," Chris says. "I'm not usually like that during trial, but I was so pissed at that defense attorney."

After Kelli testified, she was able to stay present in the courtroom to watch Chris cross-examine Kent Easter.

"It was so hard for me to sit there and listen to Kent lie and lie and lie," Kelli says. "I couldn't believe that a person like him—a wealthy attorney and previously respectable person—would stoop to this. An officer of the court, as he was, should respect the oath that he took. I was completely floored that he just sat up there and blatantly lied. It was hard for me to watch. I was disgusted."

During his cross-examination, Kent showed zero emotion.

"He was smug, snide, and cool as a cucumber," Kelli says. "He acted like he had it in the bag. It was as if this was all an inconvenience to him."

Kent had just sat through Kelli's very emotional testimony about what his and Jill's actions had done to her family, and yet nothing. Just a blank stare, as if Kelli didn't exist…as if she weren't a human being with feelings. With an arrogant manner, he continued to deny any wrongdoing.

Soon, the testimony wrapped up and it was time for closing arguments. Kelli was excited that the trial was finally coming to a close.

Chris had worked hard on his closing argument. He wanted to hit home every point to the jury.

Throughout the trial, he'd presented a brilliant, well-organized case that the jurors could relate to and understand. On top of that, he was a charismatic man with a gift for engaging directly with the jurors.

"I was mesmerized by Mr. Duff's closing statement," Kelli says. "It made me realize once again just how awful Jill and Kent were. They were guilty; it was so obvious. I thought that it shouldn't take too long for the jurors to come back with a verdict. I was so relieved that it was finally going to be over. I could feel the pressure in my head go away, and my shoulders started to relax a little. I knew Kent would be found guilty. Chris was so brilliant. The jurors were completely riveted by his closing; they listened to every word with spellbound expressions. He completely discredited Kent's story. I was one hundred percent sure a guilty verdict was just minutes away."

After Chris finished his closing argument, Kelli breathed a sigh of relief. Now the case would go to the jurors. After all the hard work by everyone involved, it was finally time for deliberation.

Kelli paced and waited for their verdict. *They need to find him guilty. Please find him guilty.*

Hours passed.

Then days.

Kelli paced at home and chewed her nails.

Finally, Chris called and said, "They have a verdict."

"What is it?" Kelli asked, her heart thumping in her chest. *It has to be guilty. It has to be!*

Chris broke the news:

Eleven out of twelve jurors had thought Kent Easter was guilty, but one wanted to give Kent a misdemeanor sentence, which was impossible. The judge tried to explain to the juror that she couldn't make that decision, that the crime was a felony, and if she thought Kent was guilty, then she had to vote guilty.

The juror had refused to budge. "I just don't feel the crime fits the punishment," she'd said.

"You can't determine that," the judge told her. "Your job is to decide if he's either guilty of the crime or not."

"Okay, then he's not guilty," the juror said.

Kelli couldn't believe what she heard.

"She didn't want Kent to have a felony, although she thought he was guilty," Kelli says, "so she refused to convict him. She wanted to rewrite the rules. She was completely taken by all the cameras in the courtroom, and it seemed she wanted fame and attention. I'm sure she hoped to be interviewed by TV reporters as the holdout juror, but no one wanted to talk to her because most everyone thought she was stupid."

"I'll Get You!"

Kelli's heart sank when she realized the juror had created a deadlock. She could hear the disappointment in Chris's voice.

*This can't be happening!*

After all those months of testimony, all of the hard work on the part of the DA's office and investigators and police, it had come down to one juror holding out.

The judge declared a mistrial.

# fifteen

When the criminal trial ended with a hung jury, resulting in a mistrial, Kelli was devastated.

"The thought of putting my family and myself through it all again was more than I could bear," she says. "The first trial had already taken a terrible toll on us. Facing Kent and his lawyer had been excruciating. Once again, I would have to dig deep and find the courage to go in and tell my story to a whole new jury."

Chris Duff reassured Kelli. "It'll be okay," he said. "We'll get through this. I have another strategy, and Kent isn't going to get away with this."

Kelli was still upset about the lone holdout juror, though. It was hard to shake for weeks.

"Had she not seen or heard what my family and I had been through?" Kelli says. "Her thought process was baffling. Everyone thought she was as crazy as Jill Easter in some ways. She truly thought she could rewrite the rules of court; it was weird. The defense attorney knew what he was doing when he chose that wild card. She didn't make any sense. One thing I've learned through all this is that there's no understanding certain people. You can't even try. It's a waste of time."

All Kelli could do was accept things as they were and move on.

She had to save her energy to gear up for another trial. Somehow, she would have to find the courage to press on.

The second trial date was set, and the DA set about presenting the case again to a whole new set of jurors.

Kelli was once again grilled on the stand by the pit-bull defense attorney. Chris once again had to present the evidence in its entirety and minutiae, and every single official who'd testified in the first trial had to do so again.

"I felt stronger this time," Kelli says. "I'd been through it all before."

Even though she had more resilience, she still cried every time she took the stand and talked about what she'd been through.

The DA saw how Kelli's very real, palpable emotions affected the jurors.

"From a prosecutor's point of view, it was powerful," Chris says. "When a victim shows honest, genuine emotion, it impacts the jury."

Finally, the trial came to a close. Once again, Chris Duff presented a riveting closing argument that captured the jurors.

Then it was time for Kelli's victim impact statement. She was at home sick with anxiety, so her Irvine PD victim advocate, Katie Zabinski, read it aloud in court instead:

*4/12/2011*

*Your Honor,*

*My name is Kelli Peters. I am the victim of Jill and Kent Easter, the defendants. I am writing this Victim Impact Statement so that you will know the impact this has had one my life and my family's life and the terror we live with every day and the emotional and financial stress we have endured.*

*On February 16$^{th}$ 2011, I was at my job at Plaza Vista Elementary. My karate instructor was running late so I was out in the*

*Multi Purpose Room with the kids who take karate and I was having them stretch etc. Mrs. Trumbaur the Administrator at the front desk came back to tell me that the police were there for me. So I went to the front to see what they needed. They told me that someone had called in and said I was driving erratically through the school parking lot at 1:15pm that day. I told the Officers I wasn't in my car at that time. I was here at the school with my classes. I said there must be some mistake. The Officer said the caller identified me by name. I was so confused. I just wasn't in my car at that time. I knew it was a mistake. I said so what now? The Officer said I need you to get your keys and go open your car. And I said for speeding? I don't understand. He said the person who called said they saw me putting drugs in my car, specifically in the pouch behind my seat. I said oh my god, what did you just say? I was completely shocked. I said there is no way that I did that, I will get my keys and show you. When I walked outside, my car was surrounded by police cars and there was a helicopter flying overhead. I just kept thinking, what the heck is going on? This is crazy, I was really freaking out. This was happening at the school and there are kids inside and my colleagues and parents and most important my daughter.*

*When we got to the car, I could see the bag of marijuana sticking out of the pouch on my seat. It was sticking out so obvious. Anybody could have seen it if they walked by. I fell to my knees. I just couldn't believe this was happening. And then the officer pulled out two big bags of pills. The feeling that came over me was a feeling of helplessness and fear. I just started weeping. I actually asked the officers if this was a joke. I pinched myself because I thought I was dreaming. I couldn't stop crying. I told them over and over that this stuff was not mine and that I have an enemy. I immediately knew who did this to me, Jill Easter. Thankfully the officers were able to do some preliminary investigating. I think they knew that this was killing me. Even though they were detaining me they walked me inside the school and let me see my daughter and call my husband. I was so concerned for my daughter. I knew she was probably really upset. When I saw her she had been crying. It was so sad. I was completely beside myself with fear and I felt so helpless. I didn't want to let her go. The police took me back to a room by the Principals office and I fully cooperated. I gave the Officers my consent to go out and search my home and they found no evidence.*

*The next day CSI came to my house to do some DNA testing on my daughter and myself. They fingerprinted my car and asked me questions. I was introduced to the lead investigator who told me that he had detectives from Irvine's specialized investigations unit coming to help. I had not slept the night before and for months after. I didn't leave my house the next day and for two weeks after without someone escorting me. I was scared and I was stressed. And I wasn't taking any chances. Neither were the police. They made sure to escort me to the school that week to do my job and we had an undercover police officer on campus watching out for anything suspicious.*

*I have a nice life, I am a happy person. My days are routine and I do a lot of volunteering at the school. It's what I love and it's what I live for. The Easters have completely taken the freedom I felt away from me. I am so shook up and so frightened all the time. I can't enjoy anything. I am constantly looking over my shoulder and in my rear view mirror. I cry night and day and I have lost 9 pounds. I can't sleep and I feel sick to my stomach all the time. I am so tired. I feel so violated. I have lost trust in other people. The stress of knowing they almost had me arrested and put in prison for something Jill Easter did to me, is too much. It's not normal to have CSI swabbing you and your daughter for DNA. It's not normal to be working with an investigator or the police on a daily basis. I* can't take this stress. It's too much for me. It feels unjust that the suspects are going on with their day to day life and enjoying their freedoms. The Easter's originally registered their children for school where they planted the drugs. I was supposed to give a speech as the new PTA president to the Kindergarten Parents and after all this I had to back out. I thought they were going to be there. I was scared. I just couldn't do it.

I am currently undergoing intense treatment for depression and anxiety. My Therapy includes a treatment called EMDR. This treatment is for patients who are suffering from anxiety or distressing memories, nightmares, insomnia, abuse or other traumatic events (Eye Movement Desensitization Reprocessing). It is time consuming and expensive but I am hoping to get some relief from all the stress the Easters have caused me.

This has not just been stressful for me. My husband and my daughter have been directly affected by their actions. My husband had to go to the doctor for chest pains and stress. He hasn't slept a full night since the day this happened. He feels helpless and afraid to leave our daughter and me just to go to work. He changed all the locks on the doors at our home and he locks the doors and sets an alarm every time he steps out the door even if it's just to go to the garage. He's had to take several days off from work to be home with me when I have bad days of anxiety. Sometimes I can't be alone or I can't get in my car to pick up my daughter or get groceries. My daughter is feeling the stress too. She is only 11 and she has been tested for DNA! She will not sleep in her bed. She was and sometimes still is afraid to go to school. We have had several meetings with school teachers and the undercover police officer to come up with strategies to make her feel safe and want to go back to school. She said to me that she felt like she was going to be kidnapped. I just couldn't believe my ears. She is so stressed out and her anxiety is like something I have never seen before. She is only 11!! No child *should feel this kind of stress. Ever! Sydnie is now having Therapy with her School Counselor so that she can hopefully regain some confidence and concentration. This situation has totally affected her school work and social skills. It is so sad. I feel so sad for her.*

*I hope when you consider this case, you take in to consideration how evil their intensions were. They wanted to see me get arrested. They wanted me taken away in a police car in front of my daughter, the kids I work with, the teachers and administrators I work with, and the parents who trust me with their children every day. They wanted to ruin my life. They wanted to see me go to prison. They wanted me banned from the school and from the district for life. They wanted to ruin me financially and emotionally. I have endured so much physical and emotional stress and pain. I have been so sick for so long. So much of my time has been spent on trying to maintain a normal life. My husband has missed so much work and spent time instead at the doctor's office or at home making sure his family is safe instead of out doing his job and making a living. We have lost money and spent money all because the suspects plotted and conspired to terrorize my family and me. I have documentation of the abuse the suspects have inflicted on me for over a year. The stress I undergo on a daily basis is something I have never experienced in my life. It is unprecedented. I need it to stop. The Easters should be punished to the fullest extent of the law. They need to finally understand they are not above the law. They should not be able to get away with the crimes they have committed and the terror they inflict upon people. It's so hard to comprehend two people being so evil and so intentionally harmful to another human being.*

*Thankfully my family, my friends, my school and the foundation IPSF that I work for never once thought I was guilty of such a horrible crime. They stayed behind me 100% because they know who I am.*

*I would like to thank the Court for taking the time to read my Victim Impact Statement. I realize your time is valuable and I am so grateful for your time.*

*Sincerely,*
*Kelli Peters*

After Katie read Kelli's victim impact statement in court, she noted the emotion on the jurors' faces. Kelli, in her statement, had opened up and bared her heart to strangers, and they'd responded. Katie called Kelli to tell her that she'd seen some of the jurors wiping away tears. This touched Kelli. It made her feel as though the jury understood what she'd been through and what she'd lost.

"It meant a lot to me that they got it," Kelli says. "They felt my pain."

The jurors convened to deliberate, and once again, Kelli was on pins and needles.

The jurors didn't deliberate long this time. In fact, Chris Duff said it was the quickest verdict he'd ever experienced.

This time, all twelve jurors came through with the verdict that everyone on Kelli's team had been hoping for: *guilty.*

Many observers in the courtroom who'd followed Kelli's plight from the beginning also wiped away tears. The DA beamed with elation.

They'd done it!

Kelli was at home when she heard the news. She hugged Bill and Sydnie as all three of them wept.

Bill was so worn out that he was barely able to say anything. He just hugged Kelli as tears trickled down his face. He'd lost so much weight in the past two years that Kelli's arms were able to wrap completely around his thin frame.

"He was so tired and weak," Kelli says. "It all had taken such a toll on him. I hugged him tightly and thanked him for being our rock and for taking care of his girls so well."

The three of them just held on to each other and basked in that moment. Justice had finally come.

"That was a great day," Kelli says. "My gratitude to Chris Duff and his team was colossal. Thanks to them, we had a confession and admission of guilt from Jill, and a conviction for Kent. It was such a victory."

In court a few weeks later, Kent Easter stood confidently before the judge with a smug expression. When he was sentenced to six months in jail and three years' probation, his shoulders slumped.

One of Kelli's friends observed, "For a moment after sentencing, Kent looked as though he wanted to throw himself to the floor in a fit of histrionics, weeping and gnashing his teeth over his 'horribly unfair sentence.' It was as if he wanted to shriek, 'But I'm the great Kent Easter. I'm a rich attorney. How could *I* possibly be going to jail?'"

Kent was then led out of court wearing a confused, stunned expression.

Everyone on Kelli's team rejoiced.

Chris congratulated everyone for a job well done. When Kelli got the news, she hugged her family and called everyone she knew. Tears flowed and cheers could be heard.

It was time to celebrate!

One of Kelli's friends threw a party for everyone who'd been part of the case.

"It was as much Chris's victory as it was mine," Kelli says. "I wanted to make sure he was celebrated and honored."

There had been two grueling trials with mountains of evidence. There had been a shark defense attorney who constantly went on the attack and kept everyone on their toes. Innumerable people had testified. Kelli had been extremely emotional during both trials and had needed a lot of comforting and guidance. Chris had been more than a DA; he'd been her confidant, friend, and therapist. He was the captain guiding a crew of saviors. During that time, he'd grown close to Kelli and her family. He'd put in countless hours to see that they received justice, and his determination had prevailed.

"We knew we had the right people and a strong case," Chris says. "But a jury is made up of twelve random people. There are no guarantees. It was such a weight off everyone to have it done."

Everyone was exhausted but happy. It had been an emotionally draining three weeks, and they all were ready to celebrate.

At the party, everyone, from the police officers, to the court advocate, to Kelli and her friends and family, ate good food and toasted with champagne.

"I got to see a different side to Chris," Kelli says. "I met his wife, I met some of his colleagues, and they were incredible people: down to earth, caring, wonderful individuals."

Kelli enjoyed discussing the case with everyone. "It was nice to finally be able to talk freely about it," she says. "Everyone had an opinion about the Easters. Hearing what everyone had to say about my case was very healing. It made me feel human. I began to feel like I really wasn't so alone because they were saying it could have happened to anyone."

One by one, those who'd helped her case came up to Kelli during the party to congratulate her and express their joy for her victory. Their relatives did so as well.

"They said things like, 'It was an honor to be part of your story and your victory,'" Kelli says. "Those trials took years, and their families had made huge sacrifices. The effort was enormous, but they were happy to do it. Every one of those people played a part in helping me and my family receive justice. To see that kind of love and commitment to their jobs and to me is something that will forever live in my heart. It had a profound impact on me."

For the first time in years, Kelli was able to genuinely smile again and feel a sense of hope and joy. She'd endured so much during the past two years, and she felt as though she'd come out of it all as a stronger person.

"A weight had been lifted off her," Chris says. "There was a psychological change. She has some grit about her now that she didn't have before. I could see that no one was going to push her around again."

Chris was also glad to see the Easters punished. "They never showed an ounce of remorse," he says. "Kent was cold and calculating and uncaring the entire time I observed him. Neither Jill nor Kent ever owned up to what they did. Ever…even despite all of the evidence. It's a forgiving country, and yet the two of them never admitted to any wrongdoing. They harmed this woman and her family intentionally and without remorse, and they did it to the nicest person on the planet. Kelli wouldn't harm a fly. That's the irony, for those two people to go after her with such intent. She, herself, would never dream of being so malicious."

Kelli and her family and friends partied at Chris's party until late that evening. Laughter and toasts of celebration rang out through the house. Kelli introduced everyone to her new civil attorney, Rob Marcereau, and his wife, Inga. Chris told Rob, "Anything you need, just call." There were more toasts to the future, and Kelli's heart ballooned with happiness.

"We were one big happy family," she says. "A team. The best team a family could ever dream of having."

It had been so long since Kelli had felt even a flicker of hope, and now she was overcome by it. She blinked back tears of joy as she watched Sydnie jumping in the bounce house and playing in the pool with Chris's children and Detective Andreozzi's children. Her daughter had a smile on her face again. There was a warmth, a camaraderie, amongst all these people that stayed with Kelli long after the trial was over.

"The only way to describe it was love," Kelli says.

When the party ended, Kelli, Bill and Syd drove home with a contentment they hadn't felt in a long time.

Things were going to be okay.

In fact, they were going to be good again.

But soon, it was time to get back to it. Kelli, after much convincing, had decided to go after the Easters for monetary damages due to the emotional distress suffering she and her family had endured. Even though it seemed daunting, it was time to roll up her sleeves and take on the Easters once again.

There was a civil trial to prepare for.

# sixteen

The entire time that Kelli was under attack by Jill and Kent Easter, she never had money to hire an attorney of her own. The Irvine Public School District had used their legal team to defend her against Jill's constant lawsuits, and then the DA had taken it from there.

"My husband and I aren't rich people," Kelli says. "We live paycheck to paycheck, like most people. Bill is close to retirement age, so the money we have is money that we need to live on as seniors. We didn't have the money to fight the Easters when they filed lawsuit after lawsuit against us. Our hands were tied from properly defending ourselves against their claims. It seemed like a game to them. They both came from money, they were wealthy attorneys, and they had unlimited resources. For them, filing lawsuits was nothing, but to us, it was absolutely devastating."

Kelli tried repeatedly over the years to hire attorneys, but she was unable to afford any of them. Nor would any of them work on contingency. They all needed money up front.

After one such meeting, Kelli left in tears. "I couldn't believe the system could let this happen. The Easters could file lawsuit after lawsuit filled with lies, and I couldn't defend myself without money. It seemed so brutally unfair. I called Bill in hysterics and said we were just going to have to do this on our own. The only thing that kept me going was knowing I had the truth on my side."

Luckily, Kelli had an attorney friend named Debra who could advise her. Another friend, Paulina, introduced Kelli to a civil attorney who agreed to take Kelli's case on for free.

Up until that time, Kelli hadn't wanted to sue the Easters. It wasn't about money to her. It was about right and wrong. It was about standing up to bullies. It was about justice.

"I told everyone that all I wanted was an apology," Kelli says. "Even after I hired Rob, I would have dropped the lawsuit if the Easters had shown remorse and said they were sorry. I was looking for any excuse to get out of it. The thought of seeing Jill and Kent Easter in court and having to go through it all again sounded like a nightmare. Those two scared me to death. They were so evil and hated me so much. By the time the civil trial arrived, they would've already served their jail time and would be extra pissed. I just wanted peace."

Bill encouraged Kelli to sue, and her friends and family promised to be there every step of the way. Kelli mulled it over. She was filled with conflicted feelings. Even though she and Bill were struggling financially, she didn't want anyone to ever have the perception that she was doing any of this for money.

Finally, after much introspection and thought, she decided to go through with the civil lawsuit.

"I needed to show Sydnie what I was made of," Kelli says. "I wanted her to see that what the Easters did to us was not okay. Because their jail time was so small, it was important to me that they were held accountable for the emotional part of this, not just the criminal. This wasn't just a normal crime where they stole our wallet. They tortured us for years. Now it was time to roll up my sleeves and face the Easter Monsters again. My family had been bullied for so long that it was now my job to go fight back. Bill was now sick, and Syd was well into high school. I needed be strong for my family."

## "I'll Get You!"

A lot of things had changed since the criminal trial. Bill was no longer the man he used to be. A week after the verdict, strong, vibrant Bill Peters finally succumbed to the stress.

"Bill got sick the week after Kent Easter was finally found guilty of all the crimes against us," Kelli says. "It took two years and two trials. It was a long and very tiring road. We were all mentally and physically exhausted. Bill, the rock of our family, the king of his castle, had a severe breakdown. He woke up one morning and couldn't figure out how to log on to his laptop computer. He hadn't just forgotten his password. He couldn't physically remember the process. I looked at him and said, 'Bill, is something wrong, honey?' He had the most confused and sad look on his face."

Bill couldn't remember other things that day as well. He was acting so strangely that Kelli immediately took him to see the doctor. Bill was tested for a possible stroke, heart attack, or brain injury. The doctors ruled out everything except severe PTSD. They wanted Bill to return for further testing.

"I took him home and put him to bed," Kelli says. "The next day he got up, sat in his favorite chair, didn't say hi, didn't go potty…just sat there. I asked him questions, and he wasn't answer me. I said, 'Are you just giving up? Why won't you talk to me? I know you don't feel good, but you have to talk to me. Bill, I need you to tell me what's wrong.'"

Bill wouldn't answer. Instead, he continued to stare off blankly into space.

"I was pleading with him," Kelli says. "I was saying, 'Bill, please. I love you. I need you to snap out of it, Sydnie needs you. Please talk to me!' I was shouting by that time. He looked comatose."

Bill continued to stare straight ahead, motionless. Kelli shouted that she was going to call an ambulance, but he still didn't react.

"I got really scared," she says. "I tried to make him get up. I was pushing him from the back and pulling his arm pulling as hard as I could, screaming, 'Bill, get up!' and he just blankly stared at me. His head began to drop forward. I dropped to my knees while holding his hand. I was pleading for him to come back to me. Then he started to turn yellow in front of my eyes. I was crying hysterically."

Bill was rushed to the hospital. The staff immediately started performing lifesaving procedures on him.

"He was minutes away from dying," Kelli says. "He was having complete kidney failure, and other organs were starting to shut down."

After two days in the hospital, Bill made it through. He would then start getting treated by a neurologist, a urologist, a psychologist, and a psychiatrist.

Psychologist Dr. Nina Rodd diagnosed him with acute trauma disorder, generalized anxiety disorder, and major depressive disorder. He was put on disability leave from his job.

"He would never be the same," Kelli says. "He would have to learn how to write his name, shave, go the bathroom, make food, and dress all over again. Jill and Kent's actions not only hurt me, but they ruined my husband's life."

The Easters had stolen the life of the robust man that Kelli had married. He was now only a shell of the person he'd been before the Easters had entered their lives.

"For that reason alone, I had to go through with the civil trial," Kelli says. "Bill deserved justice. So did Syd. The Easters had hurt our family in indescribable ways. We were living on social security and our savings. Because of what the Easters had done to us, we were essentially broke. Our hopes and dreams for ever retiring were gone. The future was so scary for us. Never in a million years did I think I would be in this position so late in life. All this emotional damage has a price tag, except there isn't enough money in the world to make any of it better. What I really would like is my old life back, but that's something I will never have. Somehow, I needed to convince a civil

## "I'll Get You!"

jury that our sad story and ruined lives were worth at least something. So I decided to go forth and try for civil damages."

She found the perfect champion in Rob Marcereau.

He was a charming, high-energy attorney with a zest for the law and finding justice for innocent victims. He'd gone to USC law school and worked as a business litigator at a large law firm, Rutan & Tucker, in Orange County prior to starting his own practice with his partner, Sy Nazif. He'd opened his new office only a month prior to meeting Kelli Peters.

"She was my first case in my new practice," he says. "I was excited and ready to take it on."

Kelli immediately felt comfortable with Rob. He walked her through what to expect in a civil trial.

On the first day of jury selection, Kelli walked into the courtroom and saw Kent Easter. He passed by her closely and gave her a cold-eyed stare that made her stomach churn.

"I used the courthouse bathroom to get physically sick," Kelli says. "I vomited in the toilet."

The attorneys saw how upset she was and sent her home to gather herself. On the way home, Kelli cried. She kept saying to herself, "I can't do this. I can't do this. I'm not strong enough. I can't do it."

Kelli drove home and went straight to bed. As she passed Bill in the kitchen, she saw a look of confusion and disappointment on his face. At that moment, it dawned on Kelli that she would also have to explain to Sydnie why she'd left court.

Kelli cried hysterically for an hour, sobbing into her pillow. It was all too much. All of the stress, all of the pressure of the past years—the harassment, the trials…it had come to this. She had nothing left to give.

And then…she caught a glimpse of herself in the bedroom mirror.

She stopped crying.

"I suddenly saw myself," Kelli says. "I was all dressed up for court in clothes I'd spent a lot of money on and spent hours picking out so I could fight these people. I had wanted to look presentable, and now my clothes were wrinkled, and I had makeup smeared all over my face. I said to myself, 'What are you doing? Get your ass out of bed, clean yourself up, and get back out there and fight those people! Think of everyone who has spent so many hours and money getting you to this point. You've already won. This is your day in court. It's time to finish this, Kelli. All you need to do is show up.' From that moment on, I was a changed person."

Kelli called Rob Marcereau and apologized for being a baby. "I'm ready," she said. "I'm ready to go hang this bastard."

After all those years of crying and sickness and worrying and loss, Kelli was not going to shrivel up and blow away now. She was ready.

"I grew a giant set of balls that night," Kelli says. "I woke up the next day ready to go. Kent Easter still made me nervous and queasy, but I just put a wall up in my mind and pressed on."

Choosing the jury for the civil trial was a difficult and time-consuming process.

"I could tell that some of the jurors just didn't want to be there," Kelli says. "It's hard for a person to take five days off from work and family. I was very uneasy because I could see how unhappy some of them were. I felt so bad. I didn't want to waste their time. I really struggled with that. I had a husband at home who needed my care twenty-four hours a day, and I was leaving him to be in court. So I knew the struggles these people had because I had them too. I was pissed at Kent for that reason. It was so hard being away from Bill. I prayed to God all day to take care of Bill. Thinking about Bill and Sydnie gave me so much strength. I needed to do this for them. I needed this victory. I would be the only one testifying for my family this time. It was time to face the enemy."

Since the trial was going to center on getting emotional distress damages for Kelli and her family, it was important that the jurors were sympathetic to victims. However, some of them were skeptical of the concept of emotional distress damages.

"I totally got it and understood their position," Kelli says. "There is a lot of manufactured 'victimhood' in the world. But some of the jurors flat out told us that they didn't believe in awarding emotional damages to people. In their minds, they thought victims should just suck it up and move on. Even though I knew how much emotional distress damages I had, would I be able to show them? Would they be able to sympathize? That is why I needed the brilliance of such great attorneys. Imagine your life hanging on the line and in the hands of twelve people you've never met before in your life. Would they believe me? Or believe the Easters' lies instead?"

By the end of the second day, the twelve jurors were picked, and everyone was ready to go.

"We were off!" Kelli says. "It was time to start the trial."

Every day after that, Kelli showed up in court ready to do what it took. Rob and his partner, Sy Nazif, walked her through her paces. It wasn't easy sitting for hours with her arthritis. Nor was it easy listening to Kent, who, in his opening statement, put her down and told lie after lie.

Kent was representing himself at the civil trial. Instead of the expensive suits that he'd worn during the criminal trial to show how rich and successful he was, he'd now taken to wearing the same old sweater day after day in court.

"He dressed like Mr. Rogers from the kids' TV show," Kelli says. "He was acting poor and penniless. It was quite the performance. He would hang his head and give sad eyes to the jury, like some starving waif. He didn't even wear a belt. He kept pulling up his pants as they fell below his ass crack. I saw his ass crack on a daily basis, and it wasn't pretty. Here was a man who'd made $500,000 a year, trying to pull a fast one over on the jury. Once again, he was showing that he thought he was smarter than everyone else. I hoped the jury would see through the charade."

Rob grilled Kent on the stand about his role in the drug planting. For every slick answer that Kent shot back, Rob had a swift and strong rebuttal.

"I'll never understand that guy," Rob says. "He lost everything for that woman, Jill Easter. After he planted the drugs, he lost his marriage, his law license, his well-paid career as an attorney, his standing in the community, his family, everything. And yet here he was, still trying every which way to get out from under his comeuppance. He never apologized. If he was smart, he would have completely fallen on his sword and said, 'I have no excuse, I loved her, I knew it, I did it, I knew it was wrong, I'm sorry, nothing I ever do or say will ever make it right, I'm here to take whatever punishment you good people of the jury will give me, I'm here to take my medicine.' If he'd done that, it would have been a lot harder for me to demonize him to the jury."

As the trial continued, Rob continued to show the jurors exactly who Kent Easter was: a liar who was not only trying to weasel out of what he'd done, but a man who had no conscience—a man who instead dismissed the pain and suffering he and his wife had caused an innocent family.

On day four of the trial, Kelli was to be cross-examined by Kent.

"My worst fears were literally in my face," Kelli says. "I couldn't sleep the night before. I was terrified of Kent Easter. He was my bogeyman. I was really disoriented that morning."

Kelli tried to have a normal breakfast with her daughter—making her food, checking on homework, getting her to school on time—but all she could think about was her day ahead in court. Bill, bedridden with a blanket around him, told Kelli how terrible he felt for being too sick to accompany her to court. His face was drawn and pale and etched with pain. Kelli hugged him and told him not to worry. She was strong. She would be okay.

"Bill wanted so badly to protect me," Kelli says. "But it was my turn to protect him. There was no way I was letting Kent and Jill get their grubby hands on Bill. He'd gone through enough, and I would protect him at all costs, even if it meant going to court alone without him. If that's what I needed to do, then that's what I would do. I had so much support from my attorneys, family, and friends. I was ready to face the Easter Monster once again."

When Kelli arrived at court, she had a quick pow-wow with Rob and his partner, Sy Nazif. They gave her a brief pep talk, and then it was time to take the stand. As Kelli was sworn in, she practiced some breathing exercises that her psychologist, Dr. Rodd, had taught her.

Kent approached the stand, and Kelli's heart raced.

"I thought I was going to have a heart attack," she says. "I told myself, 'It's going to be okay, Kelli. It'll be over soon.'"

Kent ducked his head and slumped his shoulders in a feigned pretense of being humble.

"Hi, Kelli," he said, giving her an "aw-shucks" look. "This is incredibly awkward, isn't it?" His whole demeanor said, "Ah, Kelli, don't be afraid. I'm a nice guy and won't bite."

Kelli stared at him in incredulity. *Really? A "nice guy"?* She couldn't believe his audacity. Nice guys didn't plant drugs on innocent people. Nice guys didn't destroy people's lives. Nice guys had remorse if they caused harm to innocent families. Nice guys wouldn't be able to sleep at night if they knew they'd taken a little girl's childhood away."

A bubble of anger rose in Kelli. "He was pretending to be my buddy. I was completely insulted. How dare he?"

Kent began speaking in a low, tranquil voice to Kelli, often fumbling through his words in an obvious attempt to paint a picture of submissiveness. It was clear he was trying to gain sympathy from the jury.

"He grilled me while embellishing his story constantly," Kelli says. "He minimized the amount of people who were watching me at the school when I got interrogated. He tried to make it sound like there were no kids around. He tried to discredit the amount of distance there was between my car and the front of the school to make it seem as though no one could even see me. He insinuated that I was overreacting. At one point, he made fun of the fact that I was still upset at the situation, as if I was putting on a show. I was so angry that he insinuated that. He was a monster to me. In my mind, I couldn't believe that he wasn't the one up there crying. He seemed to feel nothing at all. I mean, he'd lost everything. He'd made himself look like an idiot in front of millions of people and yet refused to acknowledge that. He just told lie after lie, and every time he told another lie, I tried not to react. All I could do was hope the jury would see through it."

One by one, Kent fired questions to her about the day Jill had confronted her, the detainment by the police, the drugs, the investigation, and what she felt she'd suffered.

"He tried to discredit me the entire time," Kelli says. "All in that fake soothing voice. He said that I was being overdramatic and that things weren't that bad. He asked, 'Why are you still crying over this? It happened so long ago.' He implied that I should be over it already. This made me furious, and I wanted to beat him at his game even more."

Rob Marcereau was hopping mad as well. "Kent Easter tried to say that what happened to Kelli was disgusting, but in the same breath he said Kelli was exaggerating and making up her pain. He said, 'This shouldn't be a winning Powerball ticket.' I said, 'Really? Look at what she won, ladies and gentlemen! She won five and a half years of misery. Her daughter won being ostracized at school. Her husband won panic attacks and the inability to work any longer and support his family. Wow, how lucky for them!' If Kent could have gone back in time, do you think he would have taken millions of dollars to put his family through this? Not a chance. For him to say Kelli was a Powerball winner was despicable and disgusting."

Kent continued to grill Kelli in a condescending way during her entire cross-examination. Kelli answered his questions coolly and calmly, although at times she was still overcome with tears. But each time the tears came, she wiped them away resolutely, took a deep breath, and squared her shoulders.

"My strategy was the same as it had always been," Kelli says, "except this time with total determination. It was: stay true to myself, remember my suffering family, stick up for myself, don't let him get to me, take the high road, and give him enough rope to hang himself. It worked."

At one point, Kent said to Kelli, "Why are you telling people you're so afraid of Jill and me? We were standing behind you at the Christmas boat parade, and you didn't seem afraid then."

Kelli snapped, "Oh really? I wasn't afraid of you? I grabbed my family together and we hightailed it out of there as quickly as we could. I was terrified of you! There were thousands of people at the parade, and you were behind me? *What were you doing behind me?*"

He said, "Well, we saw you later on Main Street and you didn't seem to mind then."

Kelli's heart dropped. "I never saw you again. You saw me on Main Street? What were you doing? Following me?" Chills ran through her body as she looked into the dark, soulless eyes of this man. He and Jill had been stalking her, terrorizing her, making her fear for her life, and now he was here, acting as if it was no big deal.

Kelli finally made it through her cross-examination by Kent Easter. She was proud of herself and felt a renewed sense of vigor.

"I don't know if he realized how badly he did with me," she says. "All I know is that every time he tried to discredit me, I called him on it, very calmly. He made himself look really bad. His strategy totally backfired. I felt good about my testimony, and smarter than Kent. When you have the truth on your side, your story never changes. Jill and Kent's story had changed so many times, it was comical."

When Kelli left the stand, she was shaky from the ordeal but felt a sense of accomplishment. She'd stayed strong for herself, Sydnie, and Bill. She'd done it.

Kelli took a seat, but she'd barely had a chance to catch her breath when Jill Easter came into the courtroom.

Jill walked to the stand in a dramatic way, as if she were a movie star on the red carpet during a press junket.

"It was entertaining from the beginning," Kelli says. "We were all there to witness what I call the Jill Easter Shit Show."

Jill took a seat on the stand, appearing eager for questioning. She wore a jean shirt tied at the waist and lots of turquoise jewelry.

"The court addressed her by all of her past and new names," Kelli says. "Jill Easter, Ava Bjork (with newfound Swedish ancestry), Ava Easter, and Ava Easterheart. She also had a sign-language interpreter in place because she was suddenly now claiming to be 'deaf.' She was also dressed completely inappropriately for court. She proceeded to tell the court that she was poor and from an Indian reservation in Minnesota. I guess she needed to dress the part, so that explained the jean shirt and fake turquoise jewelry. In my opinion, she should have dyed her hair black. Her bleached-blonde hair and blue eyes were a dead giveaway. Besides, what happened to Ava Bjork from Sweden? That had been her 'new identity' for the past few years."

Rob Marcereau began grilling Jill on the stand.

"He was brilliant," Kelli says. "It was like watching a great episode from *Law & Order*. He would ask Jill a yes or no question, and she would go off in all sorts of directions and tangents. Every time he questioned her about something specific, she would give a speech about herself, talking about her childhood and her education."

At one point, Jill pointed to every attorney in the courtroom and announced, "I went to a better law school than any person in this room."

"She was insinuating that she was smarter than everyone there," Rob says.

At Jill's words, the judge blinked and stared at her. People stifled snorts of laughter in the courtroom.

"The judge's expression was priceless," Kelli says. "I almost laughed out loud."

Another priceless moment in Jill's testimony came when she was asked about the restraining order that she'd taken against Kelli (that had been thrown out). In the restraining order, she'd demanded that Kelli stop calling her "crazy" to other people at the school.

Rob paused, looked at Jill, and said pointedly, "Have *other* people in your life called you crazy before?" Then he gave a raised-eyebrow look to the jury that wasn't missed by anyone in the court.

"My partner couldn't believe I asked her that," Rob says with a laugh, "but I went there." When asked what Jill's expression was after he asked her that question, he says, "Well, there wasn't a lot of expression on her face. Just a blank stare."

The Jill Easter Show continued. She behaved dramatically to the courtroom, and everyone was riveted by her behavior.

"My attorneys were dying," Kelli says. "We all kept looking around to see who she was playing to. There weren't cameras in the courtroom, but she sure was behaving as if there were."

During the whole trial, Jill claimed that she was deaf in what Kelli says was an obvious ploy to gain sympathy from the jurors. During a recess, one of the jurors came rushing into the courtroom.

He went up to the judge and conversed with him about witnessing Jill talking without an interpreter to her husband, which implied that she wasn't deaf after all but possibly faking it.

The judge asked, "Were there other jurors around?"

The juror said, "It was just the two of them conversing. I noticed that she had a translator when she was here inside, but she didn't have one out there. So it made me wonder."

The judge replied, "Use your common sense. You are the judge of the credibility of all the witnesses. So you take into the account what your common sense tells you to take into account. Thanks for sharing. We are in recess."

Detective Andreozzi, the lead investigator on the case, also testified at the criminal trial that his own sister was deaf, and he didn't believe Jill was because she didn't use an interpreter to talk to her extramarital lovers.

It then came time for Kent Easter to question his wife on the stand. He opened with, "Good afternoon, Miss Everheart."

Jill answered coyly, "Good afternoon."

"That was hilarious to me," Kelli says. "A minute ago, Jill Easter was Kent's wife, and now she was Ava Everheart. He was completely playing into her name change."

As Kent asked his wife questions, it was clear that they'd practiced a well-orchestrated admiration for each other.

"They were fawning over each other," Kelli says. "Boosting each other up and bragging. It was bizarre because she'd ruined his life, and yet he was looking at her so lovingly. I thought, *What's wrong with this picture?*"

Kent, leaning in and looking adoringly at his wife, took Jill through a set of questions about who she was as a person.

"She glared at me from the stand," Kelli says, "and stated that I wasn't the only parent volunteer in the room. She said, 'I have three children so I volunteer three times as much as Kelli Peters. Kids love me, and I work tirelessly to help children. All I do is cook, clean, and volunteer…that is all I do.'" Kelli shakes her head. "She certainly was doing more than that when she was having a two-and-a-half-year extramarital affair with a firefighter, which came out in court. They texted many times a day, had sex constantly at her home when Kent was gone, and had threesomes and foursomes at the firehouse. Yep, she was doing a lot more than cooking and cleaning. And she certainly wasn't volunteering. I never saw her at the school. Besides, the last time I checked, they don't allow *felons* to volunteer at elementary schools."

For every question that was asked her, Jill would answer in a convoluted way. Her story changed with every question, but she answered each with arrogance, all the while looking around the courtroom with an unreadable, frozen expression.

Rob says, "In my opinion, she came across as a liar, as very calculated, and as someone who was capable of doing and saying anything. From my perspective, she came across as terrifying. I found her to be a scary presence, and I think the jury did too. I think the jury had a lot of disgust for her and her lies. She was very condescending and arrogant."

Jill's testimony continued. Kent asked her if she'd had anything to do with the planting of drugs on Kelli Peters.

"She said no," Kelli says. "Even despite the DNA evidence, despite having been convicted and sent to jail, she was still denying it. Then she went on a rant about how she doesn't do drugs, blah, blah, blah, and how I'd ruined *her* life by spreading rumors about her. She stated that she used to be famous and now can't get a job in the U.S. because of Kelli Peters."

Kelli had had enough. She got up, scraping her chair back loudly, and walked out of the courtroom.

"I was done," Kelli says. "I couldn't believe she was saying it was *my* fault that her life was so messed up. Are you kidding me? So I walked out. The jury saw me leave, and all eyes were on me. It probably seemed dramatic, but I wanted to take the attention off Jill and her lies about me. I was done listening to her. I was *done*."

Outside the courtroom, Kelli took a seat outside the doors. Sy followed her out and placed a hand on her shoulder.

"Are you okay?" he asked.

"I'm fine," Kelli said. "I just didn't want to listen to her anymore. I'm done with her. I'll sit out here until she's done. But how can she take an oath and just sit up there and lie?"

"Don't worry; the jury sees it," Sy said. "Stay strong. It's over for her. We're just watching her implode."

Kelli said, "Then go in and watch her implode. Have fun. I'll be fine."

Sy went back in. A short while later, he returned and said that Jill was finished testifying. After a few minutes, Jill exited the courtroom and passed right by Kelli.

"She just went along her merry way," Kelli says. "She boogied on down the road without a care in the world. She probably went to get a pedicure. It seemed like such a game to her."

Then it was time for Kent's cross-examination. Kelli went back into the courtroom and listened to the judge give instructions to Kent. Then Rob began his questioning.

"I endured another grueling hour of Kent's BS," Kelli says. "But it was all worth it when Rob pulled out a copy of Jill's boarding pass to Mexico when they were claiming to be so poor. Kent had accidentally faxed it to Rob when he sent some paperwork. The fact that Jill had been claiming to have zero money yet was going to a resort spoke volumes. The look on Kent's face was priceless."

Finally, the trial wrapped up. Four days after the civil trial began, the court convened and the jury retreated to deliberate.

All that was left to do was hope...and wait.

It was February $5^{th}$, 2016, almost six years to the day since Kelli's ordeal had first begun. Was this is? Would it finally be over? As in both the criminal trials, her stomach twisted with anxiety and anticipation as she waited for the verdict. This time, however, she had a calm energy about her that she hadn't had before. She'd become a stronger woman after the criminal trials. Facing down the bogeyman—the Easter Monster—as he grilled her on the stand had been empowering.

She knew in her heart that the jurors would do the right thing, even though logically she knew there were no guarantees.

What would her suffering be worth? Syd's loss of friends, innocence, and years off her childhood? Bill's declining health? Their loss of income, savings, and retirement? All those years of fearing for their lives? The loss of all that they'd known and loved...their former lives?

"There was no price to be put on losing those things," Kelli says. "I would have given any monetary compensation back in an instant if I could have had my old life back. There was no price to be put on that kind of suffering, but here we were. A civil judgment was the only way to show the world that what Jill and Kent Easter did to us—*stole* from us—was wrong."

Less than an hour later, the jurors returned. Many of them smiled at Kelli and gave nods of encouragement, which was promising.

Then the foreman read the verdict:

The Easters were "liable" for false imprisonment and intentional infliction of emotional distress.

The jurors read the judgment:

1. *Damages to Kelli Peters for false imprisonment: $365,000*
2. *Damages to Kelli Peters for intentional infliction of emotional distress: $800,000*
3. *Damages to Bill Peters for intentional infliction of emotional distress: $365,000*
4. *Damages to Sydnie Peters for intentional infliction of emotional distress: $600,000*
5. *Joint punitive damages awarded plaintiffs against Kent Easter for malice, oppression, and fraud: $1.5 million*
6. *Joint punitive damages awarded plaintiffs against Jill Easter/Ava Everheart/Ava Easter/Ava Bjork for malice, oppression, and fraud: $2.1 million*

Total amount awarded Kelli Peters and her family for emotional suffering: $5.7 million.

Kelli burst out weeping. Some of the jurors wept as well, along with bystanders in the courtroom. The attorneys leapt out of their chairs, cheering. Everyone on Kelli's team hugged each other.

Kent Easter looked stunned.

"They fully thought they were going to hoodwink us all," Kelli says. "But the jury saw through their lies. My attorneys had poked holes in every single asinine argument they'd tried, and the jurors saw the Easters for what they were. They weren't only liars, but sadistic criminals who had created severe emotional suffering."

Kelli looked up to see the jury crying. "I was truly overwhelmed," Kelli says. "Not by the amount of the money but by the ending of an intensely life-changing, exasperating ordeal. The jurors were looking at me with such sympathetic eyes. They truly felt my pain."

Rob Marcereau says, "The judgment was an outstanding victory because of who the Easters were. These were two people of wealth and privilege, living in a million-dollar home in Irvine, living the dream. Their kids were going to one of the best schools in the world. Over something so petty and so *manufactured*, they went to extraordinary lengths to destroy someone and her family: a volunteer at the school. For years they terrorized Kelli and her family, which culminated in this drug-planting episode. But thank God for the Irvine Police Department, who performed extraordinary detective work. I think the Irvine PD was motivated to find the culprits because they were being used as an instrument of vengeance. They took this case very personally. They unraveled the thread and did some digging that other police departments might not have done due to lack of resources, time, and manpower. They immediately traced the call made by Kent Easter to the hotel and got a copy of the video. If they hadn't followed up on it immediately, the video would likely have been destroyed. And if that video hadn't been found, this case never would have been solved. Never. Kelli always would have had her suspicions, but the Easters would never, *ever* have been caught and prosecuted for this. Kelli never would have been vindicated, which is frightening."

After the judgment, Kelli looked around the room with thankfulness filling her heart.

"I was flooded with emotion," she says. "It had been years of torment and stress and anxiety and preparing and illness and sleep deprivation and worrying and health issues and anxiety…and it was finally coming to an end."

As each of the jurors left their places on the stand, they individually stopped by Kelli to say something to her personally: "Congratulations," "I'm so sorry for your trauma," "Good luck," "It was a pleasure," "Take care," "You're an inspiration," "God be with you and your family."

"One by one, they all took the time to stop and connect with me," Kelli says. "They wanted me to know that they cared. I was overwhelmed with emotion and gratitude. They knew I was emotionally wounded, and they showed me they understood by awarding me and my family emotional damages."

Rob and Sy were ecstatic over the victory. They knew it could have gone either way, although they'd been confident in their case. They hadn't expected such a huge judgment, and they were elated on Kelli's behalf.

"It's extremely difficult to get jurors to award damages for emotional suffering," Rob says, "especially ones who are already a bit jaded to begin with. But these jurors saw the truth. Kelli's an emotional person, and what she and her family went through was very real. There's no faking that. For no reason at all, the Easters made a petty but very elaborate attempt to destroy her life. It was disturbing, and I'm glad the jurors saw that."

Kelli hugged her friends who had come to support her. In her heart, she wished Sydnie and Bill were there, but she understood why they weren't. Sydnie had been through so much—she was still a little girl—and Bill was very ill. Kelli couldn't wait to get home to tell them.

Outside the courtroom, some reporters from the media converged on Kelli. She was suddenly surrounded by reporters and cameras, all asking for a statement. One of the jurors who was a clothing designer quickly fixed Kelli's outfit and hair before she went on TV for an interview.

"It was another one of those surreal moments," she says.

The jurors were interviewed as well. One of them, the biggest skeptic, said he didn't believe in awarding emotional damages to a person, but changed his mind when he heard Kelli's story. He said his heart broke when he listened to what she'd been through. After speaking to the reporters, he turned and apologized to Kelli and then hugged her.

"We hugged like that for a long moment," she says. "I was crying."

Then her friends dried her tears. It was time for her victory speech.

The first TV reporter asked Kelli what she wanted to say to the Easters.

She replied immediately: "It's not okay to bully people. It's not about money; it's about treating people like human beings."

The TV reporters clamored around her with more questions, and she answered them as honestly as she could. She was exhausted, though, and wanted to get home to Syd and Bill.

Finally, it was over. Kelli's attorneys walked her to her car, and she headed home. She pinched herself. $5.7 million! Her attorneys had warned her that she would likely never see the full amount—in fact, they said she would be lucky to receive a few hundred thousand

## "I'll Get You!"

dollars over the years—but it didn't matter. The monetary judgment was symbolic.

"The judgment was 5.7 million reasons to feel vindicated," Kelli says.

For all of his hours of work, Rob would likely not see a cent of the judgment, either.

"The Easters fraudulently hid their money," he says. "They deeded their million-dollar home as a 'gift' to Jill's father. We likely won't see the money, but the Easters are going to be looking over their shoulders for the rest of their lives. We'll be coming after every cent."

Kelli would worry about that later. For now, she'd been told by a jury of her peers that what she'd suffered had been valid.

That meant everything.

"All I wanted was a simple apology," Kelli says. "If I'd gotten that, this judgment wouldn't have happened. I didn't want a civil trial. I wanted an apology. But because they never owned up to what they did, still to this day, they will now have to pay me whatever they earn, no matter how small, for the rest of their lives. I will do whatever it takes to collect every dime from them, because now I'm mad. It's not about the money. It's about what the money symbolizes. It's about taking care of the people that they permanently damaged. It's about respect and human decency, and Jill and Kent Easter have shown me neither."

On the way home, Kelli called Syd and Bill to tell them the news. They cheered on the phone. When Kelli arrived home, they hugged each other tightly. Even though Bill was weak, he held her in his strong arms. They all cried together, their arms holding each other up. They'd made it.

Somehow, they'd made it.

After weeping for a long moment together, Sydnie finally looked up at her mom. She had tears in her eyes, but there was hope shining through in her face.

"Is it over, Mom?" she asked.

"Yes, Syd," Kelli said. "It's over."

# seventeen

In Kelli's wildest dreams, she never expected the media coverage that her story would garner. Besides local television channels, Kelli's story was featured in the following places:

*20/20, Dr. Drew Pinsky,* the *OC Weekly,* the *OC Register,* the *LA Times, Nightline, Crime Watch Daily,* the ID Channel, *Nightline, People, Momsters, Inside Edition, Good Morning America, Dr. Phil,* and the *New Yorker.*

"How did that happen?" Kelli wonders. "It was the last thing I expected. But then again, when you're dealing with people who live so outside the bounds of society, as Jill and Kent Easter do, I guess it fascinates people."

From the time Kelli had her first encounter with Jill to the final verdict in the civil trial, there were many twists and turns and unexpected events that Kelli couldn't foresee. Her life was altered in innumerable ways. One of the most unexpected changes, an aspect she'd never expected but that changed her life in the most drastic way, was the media coverage and the effect it would have on her life.

"I never expected the world to take such an interest in my case," Kelli says. "The media coverage has been overwhelming. In the beginning, I had no idea that the drug-planting incident would be so compelling to so many people. Everywhere I went, someone would stop me to talk about it. I understood the fascination locally, but to have it captivating the nation was a bit surreal."

Kelli knew she would have to succumb to doing a couple of shows after the civil trial, but there was no way of predicting that she would be asked to do *People* magazine or be on *Dr. Phil*.

"That kind of thing was reserved for movie stars," Kelli says.

The media interest first began when the Easters were arrested. Kelli did very few press interviews during that time.

"Because I wasn't out there telling my side right away," Kelli says, "there were over five years of inaccurate reporting. That was hard, because I was being told not to read anything or look at the comments. I was new to this, and I wanted to see what people were saying."

At the request of Kelli's attorneys, she was told to not respond to anything that she might see.

"There will be plenty of time to defend yourself," Rob Marcereau, Kelli's attorney, repeatedly told her. "Just be patient."

Although it was difficult to know that the Easters were saying whatever they wanted to the press, Kelli listened to Rob.

"He told me that doing press before a civil trial is a huge no-no," she says. "He's very experienced at this type of thing, and as usual, he was right.

The interest in the story never waned. In fact, it built as every month passed. The *OC Weekly* was one of the first papers to follow Kelli's story closely, and they covered it from the beginning. The reporter, Matt Coker, delved deep and always had something interesting to write about the Easters.

"Through it all, it was a huge relief when I would read something extremely entertaining," Kelli says. "Matt Coker of *OC Weekly* would keep us all up to date and in stitches on what the Easters were doing. He always had an amusing twist. He wrote some great stuff. He's very funny, and very bright."

*Good Morning America* was a show that pursued Kelli from the beginning. Before the civil trial, they offered to fly Kelli and her family out to New York to stay in an expensive hotel and have dinner at a fancy restaurant before taping.

"It was tempting," Kelli says, "but I was sticking to my guns and the advice of my attorney. *GMA* tried really hard to get us out there before the civil trial, and I always feel so bad when I had to turn someone down. I know those people worked very hard to get their stories, and I wasn't trying to be difficult. I just wasn't being allowed to do anything yet. It was for the greater good. Plus, I really wasn't ready yet emotionally."

For five and a half years, the press continued to pursue Kelli. She stopped answering her phone. Many of the TV producers who contacted her were fine with waiting until the civil trial was over to talk to her…except one.

"The show *Momsters* was the only one that didn't wait," Kelli says. "They asked to interview me, and I said I couldn't until after the civil trial. They did the show anyway. Of course, it's their prerogative, but they used my name, my likeness, and told the story from the point of view of Jill Easter. Because of that, they portrayed me very poorly. I was devastated."

At that point, Kelli had already been diagnosed with posttraumatic stress disorder, so to see herself portrayed as a villain on *Momsters* made her symptoms worse.

"It was a huge setback for me psychologically and emotionally," Kelli says. "They told the story completely wrong and made me out to be the one at fault and Jill Easter the victim. It was completely reckless. It was hurtful to me and my family. It was slanderous and irresponsible reporting."

After the show aired, Kelli was inconsolable. It took her weeks to recover, and after that, she became suspicious of the media. "I wanted to make sure that when I did interviews, they got it right."

After the civil trial was over, Kelli began to regain her strength. She felt buoyed by the civil judgment and ready to take on the media.

"I began to feel differently," she says. "I was empowered. It became easier to accept the media offers. I had more to offer, more ammo. There were so many layers to this story, but I had to wait for the final outcome in order to truly feel vindicated and ready."

The first show's offer that Kelli accepted was *20/20*. *20/20*'s cameras had been present in the courtroom during the first criminal trial against Kent Easter and had followed the story closely. It was a show Kelli watched often, and it was unnerving to know that millions of people could potentially be watching her.

"I was beyond nervous for this first interview," Kelli says. "But all the people involved with the show were amazing."

When Kelli first walked into the room filled with lights and cameras and production people, she was overwhelmed. The first person who caught her eye was Chris Connelly.

"Could this be the same Chris Connelly that I used to have a crush on from MTV?" Kelli says. "It was! I was completely star-struck."

Kelli rushed over and gave Chris Connelly a hug.

"I probably held on a little too tight," Kelli says, laughing. "Yep, I wasn't letting go. Poor guy. He was probably thinking, *Get this girl off me!* But I immediately felt relaxed when I found out that he would be the guy doing the interview. I felt comfortable with him."

Kelli's experience with *20/20* was surprisingly good.

"The whole crew made me feel so comfortable," she says. "It was my first time doing a TV interview like that, where I'm a victim and have to tell my nauseating story on national TV. What were they going to ask me? Were they going to ask about my childhood? It was so personal and invasive, and yet the producers and staff really took care of me and made me feel so good."

When Kelli cried during the taping of the show, the producers stopped the interview, then had staff touch up her makeup, hand her water, and let her gain my composure.

"I was so grateful for that," Kelli says. "I didn't want to look messy on TV. They fussed over me and that felt so nice. It took a lot to talk about my personal life to possibly millions of people. It was way out of my comfort zone. I was so nervous."

When the interview was over, Kelli called her friends and family to tell them about it. When Kelli told them that she'd just been interviewed by Chris Connelly of *20/20*, they were floored.

"No one could believe it," Kelli says. "I'm sure everyone was slightly stunned."

Soon, Kelli began interviewing with many different media outlets. Part of the pressure of doing interviews was that she didn't know what to expect. None of the producers prepped her with questions ahead of time, so she had to wing it and just answer the questions they fired at her as honestly as possible. She was used to doing this during the trials, but it still was a daunting process.

The interviews all started the same: "They would say, 'I'm sorry you had to go through this. Oh my gosh, when I heard this story, I just couldn't believe what I was reading. I mean, what the heck, these people are well educated, rich, successful, smart…it just doesn't make sense.'"

Then the interviewers would immediately ask, "What did you do to Jill and Kent Easter to make them go after you so viciously?"

To Kelli, it seemed that no one wanted to hear that she didn't do anything to provoke Jill and Kent Easter.

"It would have been a much more interesting story if it had been a catfight between two women that escalated out of control," Kelli says, "but that's not what it was. In fact, I think the story angle changed for the producers once they found out the truth. It's scary for people to know that there are individuals out there just waiting to do something to others without being provoked. It means that what happened to me could have happened to anyone. It was bad luck and being at the wrong place at the wrong time. I think that's one of the things that makes my story so relatable."

Every time Kelli was asked that question—"What did you do to the Easters?"—she would respond with a version of the following:

"I have no idea. That's the honest truth. I have no idea. I've played the scenario over and over in my head, thousands of time, and I just don't know what I could have done differently. It's hard to answer that question because I don't know what was going on in Jill Easter's head. She changed her story so many times. We eventually found out why she was late to pick up her son that day, but we don't know why she started all the accusations. She said I called her son slow, but I didn't do that. The entire situation was thoroughly investigated, and right away, it came out that nothing had happened. But Jill wouldn't let it go. She became fixated. I think that's why this story is so interesting. Ninety-nine percent of the people in this world would have handled things differently. Then there's that one percent who choose to fly off the handle, pull out a gun, or plan revenge.

"If you are unlucky enough to have to deal with that one percent, first I want to say how sorry I am for you, and second, do not engage. Document everything, and take the high road. I say this time and time again to people who ask me for my advice. If you give a crazy person enough rope, they will hang themselves. The Easters are very self-destructive—it was proven in court records how dysfunctional their marriage was—and they have no problem taking everyone else down with them. It doesn't matter who you are to them. If they can ruin a loved one's life, can you imagine what they might do to a perfect stranger? Well, I can, and it is not pretty. So the best thing you can do when encountering someone like that is run. If they persist, keep a record and keep your distance. Give them room to self-destruct. There is no need to involve yourself. Keep you and your loved ones safe, and do everything you can to stay away. It's really the best advice I can give people out there. Can you imagine what would have happened to me had I engaged in their bizarre behavior and given it back to them? Then this thing probably would have been an entirely different story, one I don't care to think about. I kept away from them, kept my family and friends close, and look what they eventually did to themselves. They are both completely ruined people and they have no one to blame but themselves."

Kelli began to accept more media offers. As she got ready for each show, squiggles of anxiety filled her stomach. She needed to have the right clothes, hair, and makeup. Some shows provided Kelli with a list of things she could and could not wear. Because she was a very casual dresser, it was difficult to find "TV presentable" outfits in her closet.

"I live close to the beach, so I dress the part," Kelli says. "Sundresses, shorts, loose shirts, colored glasses. It's really not what the producers wanted for TV. I worked with kids in an afterschool program. I didn't dress for an office. So their rules were tough for me. It was stressful."

A few of the media outlets provided Kelli a "hair and makeup person," but they changed her look so that she was nearly unrecognizable to herself.

"I looked so different from myself on some of those shows," Kelli says. "It kind of drove me nuts. I didn't feel like me, so I couldn't relax. The two shows that did my makeup were the ones I felt the least relaxed on. I was still fighting PTSD, so every little thing mattered to me. I imagine most people would love to have their hair and makeup done for national TV, but not me. I absolutely hated it."

An interview with *People* magazine came shortly thereafter.

"It was a huge shock for me," Kelli says. "I'd subscribed to *People* for years. I loved that magazine. When they called, I was floored. The media attention I got was mind-boggling. To have my story in a national magazine was just too much to bear. When it was published, everyone saw it. Everyone commented, and it was a big deal. Things like this made me feel better. It was uplifting. The magazine got the story straight from me—there would be no Jill Easter involved; it was strictly a story of survival. It was my words printed. It would be correct! No guessing what happened, no wondering what I did to provoker her, no embellishing...just my story. Again, another very surreal moment."

A few weeks later, Kelli was at the doctor's office and saw a patient in the waiting room holding up *People* magazine and reading Kelli's article. The man had no idea that the subject of the article was sitting right across from her.

Kelli leaned over and said, "Can you believe that story? It's crazy, isn't it?"

The man looked up. "Yes," he said. "Those people are really messed up. That poor girl. She looks as though she's going to be okay, though. Thank the good Lord for watching out for her."

Tears flooded Kelli's eyes. "Yes," she replied. "I think she's going to be okay. Thank God."

The magazine was everywhere that Kelli went: coffee tables, lobbies, doctor's offices, stores.

One of the best parts was when Kelli went to the grocery store that she'd been frequenting for twenty years, Albertson's. All of the employees knew her, and they were abuzz when she entered the store. They congratulated her on her civil trial victory and her article in *People*.

"I did my shopping, and then got in line," Kelli says. "I picked up one of my magazines, and it was hilarious to be reading about *me*. I talked a few customers around me into buying a copy, too. All the employees had already bought one. It was so cool."

An interview with *Inside Edition* came next.

"They were a great group of people," Kelli says. "Jim Moret and his crew were lovely. He's such a great guy, completely warm and comforting. He's a father and volunteers at his children's school. He could totally relate to my story. We talked for hours. Even his crew came up to say how sorry they were. I was so happy after this interview. I felt so empowered. We held the interview at my attorney Rob Marcereau's office with my husband Bill present. This was important because *Inside Edition* was all about making me feel comfortable."

The experience with Jim Moret and his crew was so positive for Kelli that she started to feel more comfortable with giving interviews.

*Crime Watch Daily* came next, and Kelli enjoyed the process. She was becoming more comfortable in her skin and in front of the cameras.

Then, Kelli was asked to interview with the *Dr. Phil* show.

"They'd been after me from the beginning," Kelli says, "but I never wanted to do the *Dr. Phil* show. There was no way in hell I was going to let Dr. Phil get his hands on me. Don't get me wrong, I liked his show, but in my mind, I figured he would try to find a reason for why Jill Easter had chosen me to terrorize. I felt like he might blame me in some way. I couldn't handle that. I'd done nothing wrong. She was the crazy one, but I didn't know if he would see that. He needed ratings for his show, after all."

When Dr. Phil's show contacted Kelli after the civil trial, she was still reluctant about being interviewed by him. There seemed to be nothing in it for her.

"Although I was now a 'professional' at doing TV shows," Kelli says, "I knew full well that I had zero control over the final product. Before I would give Dr. Phil my answer, I would do my homework and watch hour after hour of his show. The DA's office had already decided they were going to do the show, and I encouraged that. They'd done an excellent job with my case, and they needed their day in the spotlight. They deserved a medal! My civil attorney, Rob, was unfortunately busy with another case and couldn't go. I was still weighing my options."

Then Kelli had an epiphany.

"I'd already started writing my book with my co-author, so it struck me that if I went on the *Dr. Phil* show, maybe I could at least get him to promote our book. I needed the money, and my co-author was working for free. All of the proceeds from the book would go toward helping me and my family. My family and I were suffering financially, and I thought that was a good reason to go on the show. If Dr. Phil mentioned the book, then maybe I would start to see some income. Maybe then it would alleviate my money fears."

As Kelli contemplated whether or not to do the show, doubts ran through her mind:

*Will the show air before the book releases in August?*
*Will Jill Easter be on the* Dr. Phil *show?*
*Will Dr. Phil tell my side of the story truthfully?*

Kelli's biggest fear was that the *Dr. Phil* show would ambush her and have Jill Easter on the same stage as her. The producers promised that wouldn't happen, although they couldn't promise that they would show the book.

Kelli finally decided to do what was best for her family. She had to take a chance. If Dr. Phil showed her book, it could change everything for her. So far, she hadn't received one ounce of compensation for what the Easters had done to her and her family, and it looked unlikely that she ever would. Her book—and the *Dr. Phil* show—was her only chance.

As Kelli mentally prepared to go on the show, she tried hard to keep the anxiety at bay.

"I was a complete wreck for weeks before," she says. "Jill had turned down requests to appear on shows up to this point, but I knew the *Dr. Phil* show was one that she might consider. I couldn't handle the thought of being ambushed by her."

Kelli arrived at the studio, and she was greeted by the producers. They helped calm her anxiety and reassured her that everything would go well.

Soon it was time to go meet Dr. Phil. Kelli took a deep breath and walked out on stage. Dr. Phil shook her hand. He was a tall, large man with a kind face. He immediately made her feel comfortable.

Kelli wasn't prepared for what happened next, however.

"Nobody told me that I would also be sitting in front of a humongous large-screen TV," Kelli says. "A gigantic screen with Jill Easter's mug on it!"

Kelli's heart sank, and she immediately began to shake. "I felt as though I'd been duped."

Dr. Phil immediately started the questioning. He asked Kelli to respond to Jill's various accusations and putdowns and unfounded claims.

"She was doing it all over again, but now on national TV," Kelli says. "It was really awful. But…my book was sitting on the coffee table in front of Dr. Phil. I focused on that, and remembered why I was here. My family was suffering financially. I hoped and prayed that I could just somehow get through this interview, and that maybe at the end, Dr. Phil would pick up my book and show it to the world. So I kept my composure as I watched Jill Easter make a complete fool out of herself on national television, or as Matt Coker from *OC Weekly* would say, 'Jill Easter Laid an Egg on National TV'."

The entire time Dr. Phil interviewed Kelli, she tried to remain calm inside and keep her eye on the prize.

"Dr. Phil and I chatted for an hour," she says. "He asked me questions about Jill, and then he would say, 'Well, Jill had this to say about you.' Then he would point to the big screen where he was interviewing the shameless liar Jill Easter in all her glory. She proved herself to be deceiving, conniving, and delusional, and thank God, Dr. Phil saw right through it."

When the interview was over, Dr. Phil paused and picked up the book. Kelli's heart did a flip.

*Is he going to do it? Is he really going to do it?*

Sure enough, Dr. Phil held up Kelli's book to the camera. He said:

"I think you have an amazing story of survival, of courage, of hanging in there. Look, you have to take your power back here. That's the thing about bullies. The problem is, bullies can stop doing what they're doing, but if you take over where they leave off, and you let the scars continue, you let them alter your self-worth, your personal truth, your identity, then it's not over. Let me tell you, she tried to take you down, but by God, you're still here. And she went down. She lost her law license; she's lost her marriage; she's lost all credibility. You, on the other hand, survived. You flipped the script. Give yourself credit for that. You stood your ground, and here we are now. They wound up paying the price, not you. You, lady, are a survivor. You navigated your family through this minefield. Give yourself credit. You are a survivor!"

Kelli smiled through her tears. "I will. Thank you."

Then Dr. Phil held up her book and said to the cameras, "Buy this book."

Kelli left the show with air under her feet.

"Dr. Phil put a giant Band-Aid on my wound," she said. "He gave me hope. I'd been dying through the whole interview, which I couldn't enjoy because I'd been so blindsided. But when Dr. Phil was kind enough to hold up my book and show the world, he gave me hope. He knew what he was doing. He knew he was helping me pay my bills and take care of my family. Dr. Phil was my hero at that moment and always will be."

On May 20, 2016, shortly after the *Dr. Phil* show had aired, Dr. Drew Pinsky had guests on his show to analyze Jill Easter's interview.

Dr. Pinsky asked his guest, psychotherapist Eric Foster, the following: "She [Jill Easter] is in massive denial, has flat affect, is manipulative and evasive. Hard to know what's going on here, but something's terribly wrong, right?"

*"I'll Get You!"*

Dr. Foster replied, "I think this is a pretty classic case of borderline disorder, and the husband is clearly a narcissist. We have a borderline on our hands. Are they crazy? Yes. There's no cure for borderlines. They will do what they want to do."

Dr. Drew was quick to point out that this was an informal diagnosis, stating that they didn't know Jill Easter and were only speculating based on what they had seen from her interview.

He said, "A lot of people have borderline traits, and they don't have to be evil. Just because you're a borderline doesn't mean you have to act out on other people. But their [the Easters'] version of reality seems to beg no alternative."

It seemed everyone in the country was talking about Jill Easter and Kelli Peters.

"This time, though, it felt like people were on my side," Kelli says. "It was a nice change from all the previous years of gossip before anyone knew the truth."

Kelli's final interview took her completely by surprise. It was with David Grann, a celebrated writer for the *New Yorker*.

"This guy is a legend," Kelli says. "As we speak, he has something in production with Brad Pitt. David Gann only chooses two things to write about for the *New Yorker* every year, and he picked my story. I was very flattered by the fact that he wanted to come interview me. Unfortunately, it seemed that the real reason he wanted to do the story wasn't because of me. It was because of how crazy the situation was, and how nuts the players were: Jill and Kent. Of course, it's intriguing to try to figure it all out. David, in all his journalistic professionalism, was going to get to the bottom of it. I had to hand it to him, he had the drive. He was very nice, and from New York. A true New Yorker. We chatted for hours, and I found him to have an interesting mind. I loved getting to know him. I'm looking forward to reading about the Easters in the *New Yorker*. I am sure David will have an amazing angle."

The entire time Kelli was interviewing with national news organizations, she was still keeping in touch with reporters from local newspapers: the *OC Register* and the *LA Times*.

Kelli says, "They were my favorites. The writers, photographers, crew…they were all amazing. I appreciated the time the reporters took to get to know me and my family and get the story right. My friends, neighbors, and community reads those papers, so it was so important to have the story told correctly. One mistake could have literally ruined me. It was crucial to let people know the truth, because the story had been so misrepresented and contorted by the Easters in the past and on TV. The responsible, caring, empathetic reporting from the *OC Register* and *LA Times* meant the world to me. I will forever be grateful. I want to say more, but their articles speak for themselves."

Kelli had finally come to the end of her journey. It had been a wild one, and the media presence in her life had been a big part of it. When she was a little girl growing up in California, the last thing that she ever could have predicted would have been the events that had happened to her from 2010-2016. Little did she know that one day she would be in the fight of her life, and that the world would follow her journey with interest.

"I learned through all of this that the world is made up of good people," Kelli says. "Caring people…hardworking people who take their jobs seriously and want to do them right. I learned how much love there really is in the world. People like Jill and Kent Easter are in the minority. And for that, I will forever be thankful."

# eighteen

On March 11, 2016, one month after the civil judgment, Kelli and her family attended a party in Irvine to celebrate her victory against the Easters. The party was thrown by one of Kelli's close friends, a woman who'd been with her from the beginning. The invited guests were everyone who'd supported Kelli through her years of trauma, including all three trials.

"There was such closeness at that party," Kelli says. "We'd all come so far together, and I felt surrounded by love."

One of Kelli's friends brought a piñata to the party. When the woman walked in, a loud cheer rose up among the crowd. The cheer was followed by hoots and laughter.

On the piñata were taped the mugshots of Jill and Kent Easter.

As Kelli's family and friends gathered around to egg her on, Kelli took a swipe at the piñata. Even though she was making a show of hitting the piñata, she had mixed feelings about it. On the one hand, she wanted to whack the crap out of the Easters' faces and give everyone what they wanted. The Easters had caused her and her family six excruciating years of suffering. On the other hand, she remembered the principal's words that had been her guiding philosophy throughout the ordeal: "Take the high road."

Hitting the piñata, while funny, didn't feel like taking the high road.

When Kelli didn't break the piñata open, she handed the stick to Bill. He took a whack at the piñata as well, but was still so weak and frail that he was unable to break it open either.

Then Sydnie stepped up. "I got this, Mom." She had a look of determination on her face.

The crowd watched with bated breath as Sydnie approached the piñata. She held the bat tightly in her hands. She lifted the stick and brought it down with all her might.

*Thwack!*

The piñata burst open, spilling out its contents: PayDay and 100 Grand candy bars.

A resounding cheer went up from the crowd. Sydnie broke into a beaming smile. She handed the bat to her mom with an expression that said, "There, Mom. I just took the power back for all of us."

As everyone clapped, Sydnie bowed with a flourish. She then turned to her mom and said, "Wow, that felt good!"

Mother and daughter hugged for a long, heartfelt moment.

There wasn't a dry eye in the place.

The long journey had finally come to an end.

Jill had started it. Kelli and Bill and her team had fought the good fight and prevailed. But it was Sydnie—sweet, brave Sydnie—who'd finished it.

It was over.

Truly and finally over.

*Letter from Kelli Peters:*

For years after "the Incident," I considered myself to be the unluckiest person on the planet. My life went from a hundred to zero in a matter of minutes. I constantly asked myself what I could have done differently. Other than beating the crap out of Jill Easter on the spot, I just couldn't have changed what happened. If I could go back, I would have probably done the same thing: take the high road, disengage, and walk away. I just didn't know how to handle Jill. There is no reasoning with her, and no understanding her. She doesn't seem to have a problem leaving a path of destruction wherever she goes. As long as she feels good, no one else matters. This book was my story of my encounter with this woman. She ruined my life. I am slowly trying to recover from this damaging experience. This book is my memoir, my recollection, my side of it, and my words as told to the author. I wasn't allowed to talk for most of the five and a half years this was happening. There was an active investigation, and I was a representative of the school. I needed to keep my mouth shut, and that wasn't easy to do. I was under attack and being unjustly accused, and I wanted to scream to the world and defend myself, like any normal person would want to do. Jill and Kent Easter put all kinds of cruel, despicable slander out in the world, the school, and media. They had no problem lying time and time again, changing their stories, creating more deception. It was excruciating for my family and me to watch and hear. We suffered tremendously, every day…every minute of the day. It haunted us at night, in our sleep, at dinner, and at work. It was relentless, this constant flood of cheap shots and insults and abuse. I say that I felt like I was the unluckiest person in the world because I just couldn't make it go away. No matter what I did, it just kept coming at me. How could I be so unlucky? When would my luck change?

Well, as it turns out, I am perhaps (and I shake my head as I say this), one of the luckiest people in the whole wide world! Not because I won the lottery, not because I was born with amazing talent and ability, but because I was able to survive this horrific act against me. I didn't survive all of this by myself. No way. I learned that I had unimaginable reinforcements that I never knew I had or would ever need. I had the aid of great friends who held me up, let me use them as a crutch, and carried me through unbearable turbulence and fear. I had family come out of the woodwork to support me and brace me for a hurricane of uncertainty in the courtroom. My family always held my hand and wiped the tears away, whether in person or by phone. My family wrapped their love around me…around us. I had an amazing police department protecting me, detectives assuring my safety as they relentlessly pursued the truth. I was defended by an incredible team at the DA's office, whose wisdom, enthusiasm and brilliance shone through the onslaught of the Easters' deception and inventive fabrication their team. Chris Duff and the DA's office a hundred percent believed in bringing justice to my family and me, and they stopped at nothing to do that. I also had the most amazing civil lawyer a girl could ever ask for. Rob Marcereau and his team took us under their wing and protected us, guided us, gave us incredible strength and courage, made us feel like we were human beings, made us feel worthy, gave us hope where there was none, and shrewdly, fearlessly, and dauntlessly took us to victory. I don't think the Easters knew what hit them when we were done with them. My team, my friends, my family, my attorneys, the DA's office, the police department…they all worked together to receive justice on my and my family's behalf. The Easters announced time and again how they were smarter than everyone. Well, we are all living proof that once again the Easters lied.

I want to thank everyone who helped my family and me get through this mess. I want to thank each one of you personally. There are so many of you. You know who you are. Each person who helped did so in their own special way. Some of you baked me a cake, did my hair, or prayed for me. Some of you gave me great advice. Others gave me invaluable legal advice. Some of you threw me parties, called to cheer me up, sat in court to cheer me on, or walked with me in the mornings when I was too scared to walk alone. Some of you let me vent and cry on your shoulders, walked with me in the afternoons, and supplied me with doggy poop bags because I was so forgetful.

Some of you gave me a place to park at the beach, the only place I could unwind and de-stress. Some of you came with me to the beach. Some of you stayed with me, by my side at school, after school, before school. Some of you met me every day at the dog park and let me tell my story. Some of you introduced me to the most amazing professional people I will ever meet, the very people who helped me through this and still help me to this day. I want to especially thank the author who wrote this book with me. Your intuitive nature, fearless attitude, and incredible knowledge helped me dig down deep and find my soul again, and sometimes kept me from jumping off my balcony.

I love all of you. I owe you all my life.

Please go hug your kids.

Peace,<br>Kelli

To connect with the author, please visit

# RileyJFord.com

Printed in Great Britain
by Amazon